Blessing
of the
Animals

Blessing
of the
Animals

A Guide to
Prayers & Ceremonies
Celebrating
Pets & Other Creatures

DIANA L. GUERRERO

Sterling Publishing Co., Inc.
New York

Library of Congress Cataloging-in-Publication Data Available

10 9 8 7 6 5 4 3 2 1

Published by Sterling Publishing Co., Inc.
387 Park Avenue South, New York, NY 10016
© 2007 by Diana L Guerrero
Distributed in Canada by Sterling Publishing
℅ Canadian Manda Group, 165 Dufferin Street
Toronto, Ontario, Canada M6K 3H6
Distributed in the United Kingdom by GMC Distribution Services
Castle Place, 166 High Street, Lewes, East Sussex, England BN7 1XU
Distributed in Australia by Capricorn Link (Australia) Pty. Ltd.
P.O. Box 704, Windsor, NSW 2756, Australia

Sterling ISBN-13: 978-1-4027-2967-6
        ISBN-10: 1-4027-2967-7

For information about custom editions, special sales, premium and
corporate purchases, please contact Sterling Special Sales
Department at 800-805-5489 or specialsales@sterlingpub.com.

Dedicated to the memory of C.E.
and to the furred, finned, feathered, and scaled creatures
of this earth ... thanks for blessing my life.

Author's Note

Within this book you will find an assortment of tidbits gleaned from my own experiences, news reports, private parties, theologians, and various expert sources. In some cases, the names and stories have been combined or altered to maintain anonymity.

The intention of this work is to celebrate the divine creation of animals. Prayers and ceremonies are personal. Please use those contained within this book in alignment with your specific tradition, or belief system, and honor those rituals of others.

For additional resources related to animal blessings, products mentioned within the text, or to receive additional bonus material visit www.blessingoftheanimals.com and enter promotional code BA06DG04.

Dear Heavenly Father, Divine Mother, Beloved Spirit everywhere present, we gather together today to ask for a blessing. We give thanks for the life we enjoy and for the elements, plants, and animals that are part of our daily existence. May we live in harmony with one another, and may the blessings contained within these pages be carried throughout the world.

Contents

INTRODUCTION
Animal Blessing Adventures

Over the past ten years, animal blessings and related ceremonies have increased dramatically. According to theologians and spiritual teachers, this important trend builds a bridge between belief systems. Practices honoring pets change human viewpoints. They rise above doctrine, rituals, and practices. Pet-related events attract people of all faiths and from all walks of life.

My animal blessing experiences certainly reinforce those theories. Each venue also reveals a unique style and flavor. During my book tour for *What Animals Can Teach Us about Spirituality: Inspiring Lessons of Wild & Tame Creatures,* participation in these fun and uplifting blessings topped my list of favorite activities.

Animal Blessings: A Brief Overview
Although contemporary critter celebrations may appear novel, the tradition actually has a long past. History reveals animals featured in art, architecture, and folklore and revered in religions of all types. Animal attributes and allegories commonly found in religious works

and sacred practices are not new. Today, novelty exists in the degree and scope of pet blessing practices and related services.

Animal blessings are said to reach back to the fourth century. Creature celebrations have been noted in cultures, religions, and spiritual traditions since then, but a resurgence of interest really began in the 1970s and has heightened in this millennium. Animals as teachers and guides and similar spiritual topics now attract serious interest from the media, publishers, spiritual leaders, and religious organizations.

In November 2003, the American Academy of Religion (AAR) discussed animals in religion at their annual conference. Founded in 1909, AAR is the world's largest association of academics who research or teach topics related to religion. The Animals in Religion group remains a popular committee within the membership of AAR.

In mainstream society, animal spiritual topics attract serious attention. Even the *Wall Street Journal* has featured articles on animals within religious centers. As animal blessing trends increase worldwide, articles and segments on this topic appear more frequently within the United States and other countries.

Throughout history, animals have played important roles in art and literature and in the daily lives of humans, but speculation exists as to exactly when animal blessings and related nature ceremonies began. Anecdotal accounts surface frequently, but actual documentation is scarce. Traditionally, rural churches held blessing ceremonies for animals on farms, but today a large percentage of animal blessings occur in conjunction with feast days of San Antonio de Abad and St Francis of Assisi.

Blessing of the Animals is a compendium of stories, prayers, ceremonies, and tidbits designed for animal lovers and for those wanting to celebrate pets. Like a small treasure chest, these pages contain tiny gems designed for individual appreciation. Each jewel reflects light onto a different facet of each topic within.

Each section includes a wealth of information. "Animals Invade Spiritual and Religious Centers" delves into the history and traditions of animal blessings. Stories from trendsetting events grace this section, along with prayers and tidbits from ceremonies found throughout the world.

"Rites of Paws-sage: Muzzle Tov!" explores the pet mitzvah phenomenon. Short snippets talk about meow, bark, and equine mitzvahs. Suggested blessings and stories enhance this section.

"Muttrimony and Other Pet Nuptials" looks at pet weddings. Pet participation in human weddings is increasing, while fur flies over muttrimony, cat ceremonies, and interspecies activities. Find fun activities and vows included here.

"Pet Parties: A Pawsitive Fur-nomenon" introduces the zany and fun pet paw-ty craze. Discover unique seasonal celebrations and galas. Get the real poop on pet pageants, yappy hours, meow mixers, and beastly registries.

"Grave Topics at Tails End" reveals the latest trends related to pet loss. Learn about pet hospice and perpetual care, and find unique celebrations of life, as well as eulogies and prayers.

"Pet-pourri" completes this volume with expert tips and hints supplying additional nuggets for successful animal ceremonies.

Please visit www.blessingoftheanimals.com for bonus material on beastly blessings, pet mitzvahs, wild kingdom weddings, pet party planning, and companion animal loss.

In closing, thanks for joining me on another armchair adventure. Enjoy and revisit the content over and over again. Share it with friends, neighbors, schoolmates, families, and kindred spirits.

PART ONE
Animals Invade Spiritual and Religious Centers

oly Cow" takes on a completely new meaning during events commemorating Blessing of the Animals, World Animal Day, Animal Welfare Sunday, Earth Day, Be Kind to Animals Week, and other imaginative celebrations.

Although many of these galas look like pet shows, critters gather together alongside humans at churches, synagogues, spiritual centers, animal shelters, and pet businesses to make a joyful noise. Unique blessing events increasingly attract a wide variety of participants worldwide.

The pet blessing phenomenon, prominent in the United States, also appears in other countries in similar animal companion celebrations. What has sparked this surge of interest in animal blessings and pet galas?

The answers vary. Some cite a renewed religious interest in animals due to a return to the roots of religious traditions, where animals held a revered position. Others believe the pursuit was sparked by the environmental movement or an increased interest in animal rights. Perhaps the catalyst is a combination of all of these and more.

Activities coincide with shifts in human-animal relationships and other social changes. Although celebrated for centuries, the transformation of animal blessings and pet ownership really took hold as humans transitioned from agricultural lifestyles to urban environments.

This change gained momentum in the twentieth century as critters working on farms began to move into the homes and hearts of humans. Now, American homes with pets outnumber those without. In fact, the most recent National Pet Owners Survey, conducted by the American Pet Products Manufacturers Association, a nonprofit pet industry organization, found 63 percent of U.S. households include pets. This contrasts with previous U.S. statistics showing 30 percent of American households include children younger than 18 years of age.

The number of pet households, buying habits, and behavioral trends of pet parents prompt further cultural changes. And these have given rise to a multitude of new services and businesses catering to pampered pets and their owners. Studies conducted in both the United Kingdom and the United States indicate a trend toward increased interest in pets and increased spending for companion animal products and services.

Members of the clergy who want to reach this audience have piqued their participants' curiosity by extending family services to include household creatures, intentionally attracting animal enthusiasts through unique services with clever names, such as "Hymns and Hounds" or "Nearer to God than Fleas."

Hymns and Hounds, Florida

Hymns and Hounds was the brainstorm of minister Dee Renda. Ordained in 1983 by Evangel Fellowship International, her ministry follows an inspired path. She says, "God has a season for different things." But it wasn't until 2005 when her work really began to go to the dogs.

Her canine congregants literally get out of the doghouse by accompanying human escorts to worship services. Simple monthly services began in Apopka, Florida, under a tent. Reverend Renda said, "Hymns and Hounds is now in Absolute Heaven," referring to the pet spa and resort where services currently take place in Orlando, Florida.

Following sermons, human and non-human attendees socialize and snack during a "yappy hour." As an extra perk, Reverend Dee provides dog-training tips to those in need. When questioned about her congregation she said, "Our contemporary ministry attracts people who don't like traditional church and so provides a place of worship where people of like interests come together. In our case, the common interest is dogs."

Each Hymns and Hounds service includes a dog-centric scripture reading and teaching. Singing takes place prior to any message. Her favorite memory? When a canine congregant broke out in song to accompany the minister's solo performance. Although the owner cringed, Reverend Dee laughs with glee when she shares the story. Isn't the whole idea to sing praise to God? Pet participation just reflects her favorite passage, "Let everything with breath praise the Lord."

PET BLESSING
God bless this pet of yours.
May your love of this animal be a constant reminder of
God's love for you and all of creation.

✦ ✦ ✦

Furred, Feathered, Scaled, and Finned Blessings
Like the Hymns and Hounds ministry, more religious institutions and businesses seek to attract new members through pioneering programs for furred, feathered, scaled, and finned family members of congregants or customers. Some innovators provide prayer or visitation to ill or injured animals; a few provide candle-lighting and eulogy services for pets.

Dr. Laura Hobgood-Oster, assistant professor of religion and philosophy at Southwestern University in Texas, studies trends of animals in religion. Her research reveals an increase in these ceremonies and a trend of interfaith cooperation for animal blessings.

ANIMAL BLESSING
May we develop kinship with all living things.
Allow us to reunite with all our relations, the animals.
Let us hear the call of the earth and the beckoning
song of nature, and answer with our hearts.
Make us aware of our similarities, our sameness.
Help us recognize each unique thread of the cosmos,
and so recognize our connection to each other.
Henceforth, may we remember to honor and cherish
every living thing.

✦ ✦ ✦

St. Francis Episcopal Church, Connecticut

Canine and cat congregants get serious attention at pet-friendly St. Francis Episcopal Church, in Stamford, Connecticut. This house of worship noticed an increase in attendance immediately after one parishioner first brought her dog, Grantham, to a regular service. More people followed that example by bringing pets to church.

Reverend Mark Lingle said, "Worship with a pet is very important to those attending special services because their pets mean a great deal to them and are vital parts of their lives. Holding a pet service with pets reminds us of our connection to the larger creation and the innocence, humor, and joy that are part of the created order."

BIRD BLESSING

We give thanks for the birds of the air, those winged
*   wonders of the sky who continually engage our senses.*
We ask that our avian brethren be blessed.
Fill their nests with healthy fledglings.
Keep them sheltered from the elements.
Provide them with abundant food.
We send our heartfelt gratitude for their serenades and
*   playful antics.*
We give thanks for their gift of song, for their beauty
*   and grace.*
Bless the birds who live with us and who surround us.
May we long enjoy their graceful presence.

✦ ✦ ✦

Dog Chapel and Remembrance Wall, Vermont

Stephen and Gwen Hueneck's Dog Chapel connects people to nature and pets. Built to reflect the style of the 1820s, and completed in 2002, this small, nondenominational church located in St. Johnsbury, Vermont, affirms the connection between art, nature, life, and love. This heartfelt endeavor began during Stephen's recovery from a life-threatening illness. He said, "The idea popped into my head and wouldn't leave. … I saw myself walking inside, bathed in the light of my stained glass windows, dog carvings surrounding me, music playing. …"

Dog Chapel overlooks a 400-acre panorama and sits atop the affectionately monikered "Dog Mountain." Although Dog Chapel does not conduct services, the Huenecks say each visitor brings his/her own beliefs to the chapel and to the annual activities held there. Their motto? *"Welcome, All Creeds, All Breeds, No Dogmas Allowed."*

Another popular feature is the Remembrance Wall, where pet owners commemorate precious pets. Although no funeral services take place at Dog Chapel, people often meditate inside or ponder departed pets under a nearby tree. Many bring closure to the loss of beloved companions after they put poems or photos there.

What Dog Chapel and other religious institutions have discovered is that animals can be the bridge to help people to reach over religious barriers and find common ground. Different paths celebrate a variety of traditions, but today more and more include activities to attract animal lovers. Those participants vary in faith or spiritual backgrounds.

PRAYER FOR PET FAMILY JOURNEY
We give thanks for another day and for protecting our way.
Keep us cushioned in your shelter.
Deliver us from all danger and peril.
Safeguard us throughout our journey.
And continue to light our path until we safely return home.

MULTITUDE OF BLESSINGS ❧ Dr. Laura Hobgood-Oster, co-chair of the Animals and Religion committee of the American Academy of Religion, and author of *Holy Dogs and Asses: Animals in the History of the Christian Tradition*, sourced a rare document referencing an animal blessing held in Rome during the 1930s. Descriptions depicted large numbers of animals congregating in the piazza of St. Eusebius for a "Benedictio equrorum aliorumve animalium."

References to countryside blessings endure, documenting thousands of animals turning up to receive benedictions. Dr. Laura estimates hundreds, if not thousands, of organized animal blessings occur annually throughout the United States.

Saint Anthony de Abad

Tales indicate that the current Western animal-blessing traditions originated in Italy. Associated with St. Anthony, the patron saint of the animal kingdom, these were probably the historical antecedents of blessing ceremonies performed in England, Switzerland, Austria, Spain, and Mexico.

St. Anthony of Abad (251–356 C.E.) was also known as St. Anthony of the Desert or St. Anthony of Egypt. Blessings during the feast day of this monk take place on the Sunday closest to January 17th, the date of Saint Anthony's physical death but celebrated as his birthdate in heaven.

In Rome, an annual religious service called the Benediction of Beasts is performed near Santa Maria Maggiore. This benediction lasts for several days because citizens and visitors across the social strata send livestock and pets for blessings at St. Anthony's shrine. The belief is that when animal attendees are sprinkled and sanctified, they receive the additional protection of the saint.

ANIMAL AWARENESS BLESSING
by the Anglican Society for the Welfare of Animals
Bless, O Lord, these creatures, and all who are involved
*   in their care and protection.*
May our awareness of their needs make us sensitive to the
*   needs of every creature, for we ask this in the name of*
Jesus Christ our Lord.
Amen.

✦ ✦ ✦

REAL LEGAL EAGLES ⚜ At one time, animals on the European continent were governed by law and held accountable for their actions. Domestic animals received trial in criminal courts, where punishment upon conviction was death. Their wild counterparts fell under the jurisdiction of the ecclesiastical courts. Punishments rendered included banishment, death by exorcism, and excommunication. The Church retained full power and authority to exorcise, anathematize (curse), and excommunicate all things animate and inanimate. People prayed to St. Anthony for intercession on behalf of those unfortunate creatures.

Saint Francis of Assisi

Although many saints are associated with particular animals, Saint Francis of Assisi (1182–1226) is most closely associated with the popular trend of animal blessings. During or near October 4th, the feast day of this patron saint of animals and the environment, a significant number of animal blessings take place.

St. Francis developed a profound connection with living things through his fascination with nature. His main inspiration came from animals. He viewed animals as living examples of spiritual integrity, blessing them and striving to understand and connect with them. St. Francis is remembered for his love of all creatures, especially birds, and is probably most known for his "Canticle to the Creatures" and "Sermon to the Birds."

One famous legend about St. Francis concerns a wolf who killed and consumed both animals and humans in the village of Gubbio. In this story, St. Francis intercedes and convinces the terrifying brute to change its ways. The tale ends with St. Francis accompanying the animal to the village, where reconciliation takes place. All parties agree to live in harmony. Peace reigns between man and beast thereafter, and the creature ultimately dies of natural causes.

SERMON TO THE BIRDS (circa 1220)
by Saint Francis of Assisi

My little sisters, the birds, much bounden are ye unto God, your Creator, and always in every place ought ye to praise Him, for that He hath given you liberty to fly about everywhere, and hath also given you double and triple raiment; moreover He preserved your seed in the ark of Noah, that your race might not perish out of the world; still more are ye beholden to Him for the element of the air which He hath appointed for you; beyond all this, ye sow not, neither do you reap; and God feedeth you, and giveth you the streams and fountains for your drink, the mountains and valleys for your refuge and the high trees whereon to make your nests; and because ye know not how to spin or sow, God clotheth you, you and your children; wherefore your Creator loveth you much, seeing that He hath bestowed on you so many benefits; and therefore, my little sisters, beware of the sin of ingratitude, and study always to give praises unto God.

Olvera Street, California

Olvera Street, known also as El Pueblo, is the location of one of the oldest animal blessings in the United States. Located in the heart of Los Angeles, California, this small village attracts over two million visitors a year. Although this annual animal blessing became popular around 1930, Dr. Laura Hobgood-Oster, an expert on animals in religion, researched U.S. blessing events and believes it may actually reach back to 1781 and the founding of Los Angeles.

In the early days, when Los Angeles was a tiny pueblo, Angelinos journeyed miles to attend mass at Mission San Gabriel. In response to local appeal, many rancheros donated cattle to raise funds for the Biscailuz Building nestled near El Pueblo's Plaza Park. Once constructed, locals ceased traveling long distances solely to attend mass.

This annual tradition began as a blessing for the fertility and health of livestock. Then it expanded to include pets and matured into a magnet for animal lovers of all types. This blessing has been well attended since its inception.

Initially, Olvera Street hosted the blessing in January. However weather challenges early in the year eventually motivated coordinators to move the celebration date to coincide with Sabado de Gloria, the Saturday before Easter Sunday.

Today it boasts a large gathering of livestock, zoo animals, and cherished pets with many thousands turning out for the festivities. Religious and political leaders gather to give thanks for the gifts animals bestow on the lives of Angelinos. Animal rights groups and animal advocates set up information booths, and entertainers perform for the crowd.

Animal participants include everything from barnyard dwellers, such as chickens, ducks, rabbits, and pigs, to the more exotic—zebras, camels, brightly colored parrots, and other zoo animals. They join household pets to parade through narrow streets of the Mercado (marketplace). Some walk on a leash, others are carried, while many arrive housed in elaborate carriages, pens, and strollers.

Fine ribbon and other adornments decorate the chariots of pampered pets and beautify the cherished creatures themselves. However, the celebrated cow appears as the honored processional leader. Decked out in an elaborate cascade of flowers or a beautifully constructed mantle (ornate blanket), she traditionally leads, even walking before the Cardinal of the Roman Catholic Archdiocese of Los Angeles. This tribute honors the historic role cattle hide, meat, and tallow played in establishing a place of worship in El Pueblo.

Over the years, Cardinal Mahony has developed a unique blessing technique that must be experienced to be appreciated. Water cascades over the crowd as every participant receives a blessing; some get drenched in the process. Cardinal Mahony's participation with Olvera Street's animal blessing began upon his arrival at the Archdiocese of Los Angeles, and it remains one of his favorite events.

LIVESTOCK BLESSING

*We come together to ask for a blessing of this land
and these animals.*

*Richly bless the earth, the crops, and the livestock of
this ranch.*

*May all be fruitful and multiply in alignment with
the cycles of nature.*

Enable us to be good stewards of creation.

Keep us grounded and insightful.

Increase our knowledge and skills.

Impress us with new opportunities.

Surround us in peace.

Sustain our wonder of the natural world.

Connect us to the world of spirit.

✦ ✦ ✦

BLESSING FOR THE ANIMALS

as recited by Cardinal Roger Michael Mahony,
from the 76th anniversary of Olvera Street's
blessing of the animals

*"Almighty Father, we bless these animals for all they have
done in supplying our food, in carrying our burdens, providing us with clothing and companionship, and tendering
a service to the human race since the world began."*

BOHEMIAN BLESSINGS ❧ El Pueblo's Blessing of the Animals includes a long, diverse procession of animals with their human caretakers. Bohemian artist Jirayr Zorthian and his family began participating in Olvera Street animal blessings around 1946. Although Jirayr passed away in early 2004, the family continues to attend.

The Zorthian clan annually displays 20–30 animals including pigs, goats, geese, chickens, ducks, and other creatures drawn in garland-clad carts. Dabney Zorthian enjoys the diversity and warmth of Mexican merchants and says her favorite memories involve the children, Barry, Seyburn, Toby, Alan, and Alice. "They rode in side-baskets draped over the backs of donkeys and when older, steered the pony cart during the procession."

Family friend, Nobel Prize winning scientist Richard Feynman, and wife Gweneth, often helped decorate carts in preparation. Dabney said, "The Olvera Street animal blessing is an eclectic mix of people. Artists, scientists, and people of many faiths attend. Once, a surprised fan asked Richard if he was Catholic. He replied, 'No, I'm not—but the animals are.'"

Holy Spirit Catholic Church, Louisiana

The newest flurry of blessing events stems from a few trend-setting churches. One such innovative place of worship is Holy Spirit Catholic Church in New Orleans, Louisiana. Monsignor Roy began holding a blessing of the animals in 1972 and jokingly says he has since earned his degree in "Holy Waters Skills," also known as "Sprinkling 101."

This creature feature varies from most other blessing events, because animals and humans remain seated in one place. The service opens with music, followed by a sermon and then the pet blessing. The clergy team, a minister and deacon, circulate through the crowd. Pet attendees beyond dogs and cats often include goldfish, birds, snakes, horses, hamsters, and even a favorite iguana.

Monsignor Roy said, "The animals start out noisy but once the service begins, they quiet down. What I find interesting is that native species of critters also get still—even the wild crows." However, he concedes that some canines bark in response to being splashed between the eyes with holy water. Locals affectionately dub this service, "Dog Mass," and hundreds turn out with furry friends.

In addition to the animal blessing, Holy Spirit Catholic Church provides specialty services for animals. In response to the requests and needs of their congregation, clergy pray for sick animals. At present, no pet home visits take place, since clergy carry a heavy enough load with human congregants. However, they provide bereavement services for pet owners and often compose special pet prayers on request.

PRAYER OF SAINT FRANCIS

Lord, make me an instrument of your peace,
    where there is hatred, let me sow love;
    where there is injury, pardon;
    where there is doubt, faith;
    where there is despair, hope;
    where there is darkness, light;
    where there is sadness, joy;
O Divine Master, grant that I may not so much seek
    to be consoled as to console;
    to be understood as to understand;
    to be loved as to love.
For it is in giving that we receive;
    it is in pardoning that we are pardoned;
    and it is in dying that we are born to eternal life.

Cathedral of Saint John the Divine, New York

In 1985 the Cathedral of Saint John the Divine, in New York City, began holding its animal blessing. Thousands of people and animals attend this service, making it one of the largest blessing ceremonies in the United States. The Holy Eucharist and Procession of Animals takes place from late morning until early afternoon, but participants arrive hours before services begin.

The cathedral, deluged with humans and animals, fills to capacity, and lines form over several blocks. Readings from many sacred texts of different faiths follow the mass, but the pinnacle of the service occurs when the great bronze doors are opened and during the subsequent pageant.

Silence falls over congregants as large and unusual beasts enter the sanctuary to gather at the altar. The diverse procession includes a variety of species. Attendees may glimpse a camel, llama, cow, elephant, eagle, monkey, miniature horse, or parrot. Other unique creatures include skunks, vultures, beehives, tarantulas, and even algae! Worshipers pray together, the bishop blesses the creature crowd, and then the entire gathering exits. Once outside, critter companions receive individual blessings at several stations.

Visitors then participate in the animal fair exhibition with vendors and activities for children and adults, such as concerts, theater performances, puppet shows, face painting, food, a petting zoo, mask making, and more.

This massive festive occasion is devoted to all of God's creatures and attracts a wide variety of animal participants. Dedicated volunteers, forming one of the best "poop patrol squads," follow behind procession members and scoop up anything elephants, camels, and other beasts leave behind.

PRAYER FOR BLESSING
OF THE ANIMALS

by Monsignor Sean Flanagan

To the God who loves each of us with no conditions,
*   we come before you this day in thanksgiving for the*
*   gift of all creatures.*
We are a people of many faiths and religions.
We thank you for the gift of our diversity.
May we find unity in the variety of life.
In particular, we thank you for creating all the animals
*   that walk the earth.*
They are a reminder to us of the sanctity of creation and
*   the reality that animals have no denominational lines.*
May we learn from their example.
May all the animals of the planet be a reminder to us
*   that peaceful co-existence can be a reality.*
We pray now for more peace in our world and a blessing
*   upon this water.*
May this holy water bless the animals with the love of
*   God, and may we treat them with care and generosity.*
Amen.

Duke Chapel, North Carolina

Duke Chapel's animal blessings may be the only ones to take place
on the grounds of a major university. Once a year, since its inception in 1989, a processional marches, banners held high, into the
quad in front of the Gothic church.

Early on, the Duke interfaith service attracted other traditions
including Hindu, Jewish, Native American, and practitioners of
other spiritual disciplines. Only recently has the service become
more Christian in focus. The Duke goal is to share messages about
the importance of nonviolence toward all creatures.

Four ordained ministers recite blessings while a flute ensemble
or single flautist performs during the processional. Another out-
standing feature is the participation of the Durham Children's Choir
for anthems. The celebration even includes liturgical dance.

Duke Chapel encourages people to bring farm animals and
includes teachings about the plight of animals used for food and
research. Their underlying goal is to develop awareness of animals as

a special part of Creation and about the intrinsic value of animals, not simply what they give humans.

DUKE CHAPEL BLESSING

O sweet maker of all, we ask your blessing on every
creature gathered here today, the large and the small.
May they live peacefully in praise of you.
Bless us all to love your creation, and revere its sacredness.
We ask this blessing in the name of the one who was,
is, and always will be, our Creator, to whom every
creature belongs.

✦ ✦ ✦

St. Boniface Catholic Church, California

In the tradition of Franciscans, Father Lotito of St. Boniface Catholic Church in San Francisco, California, celebrates creation during his blessing of animals. He said, "St. Francis saw all creation—humanity, animals, the environment, plants, trees, flowers, the sun, moon, stars, water, wind, air, all the earth, and all creatures as good. All creation reflects God's love, providence, and beauty."

Father Lotito is joyful. His blessing reflects delight and may be the only one on record to blast Motown instead of hymns. "We Are Family" is his song of choice. His annual animal blessing literally has people dancing in the streets—where it takes place.

CREATURE BLESSING
as recited by Father Floyd A. Lotito
God, maker of all living creatures, we ask you to bless these
animals, and enable them to live according to your plan.

✦ ✦ ✦

Tumpek Kandang, Indonesia

Most animal blessing events welcome all species, wild or tame. Throughout Europe and the United States these historic traditions are simply called "Blessing of the Animals." In Indonesia, Hindus celebrate Tumpek Kandang (also known as Tumpek Andang or the Saturday for animals) in honor of household animals such as cows, pigs, chickens, ducks, dogs, and birds. During this special Saturday, rituals are held on farms and compounds around the country. Many animals are honored with their own specific ceremonies.

In appreciation for their assistance on the farm, cattle may receive distinctive treatment such as ceremonial bathing, specialty meals, unusual snacks, fancy costuming, cosmetic grooming, or adornment with trinkets. Creatures also receive special prayers, complete with a sprinkling of holy water or rice.

One Bali resident reported the blessing group, ". . .arrived with holy water, incense, collars woven from lontar palms, foodstuffs, and sticky white rice." The animals sensed a change in energy and calmed down, allowed adornment with handmade collars, tolerated anointment with holy water, endured wafting with incense, and permitted rice application to their foreheads.

FARM ANIMAL BLESSING

Lord of the field, pour out an abundant stream,
*   flowing thick as honey, rich as butter.*
Lord of the sky, shower us with grace.
May the air be full of sweetness, heavy with dew.
Energize us with herbs and fruits of the field.
Lords be good to us and guide us.
May our animals work heartily.
Give us joy in our labor, and let our plow yield
*   a ripe harvest.*

✦ ✦ ✦

Blessing of the Horses

The Blessing of the Horses is a species-specific tradition held throughout the year in France, Switzerland, and Italy. Even the Roman calendar contained two days to honor Calgary horses. In the United States, one of the oldest annual equine blessings takes place at the Mission Santa Inés and coincides with the annual ride of Los Rancheros Vistadores de Santa Inés.

The Rancheros Visitadores (visiting ranchers) is an elite social club that meets the first weekend in May. Founded in 1930 by John Mitchell, membership in this legendary riding group is by invitation only. Members include politicians, celebrities, and professionals from throughout the United States and beyond. Among the hundreds of past ride members and participants are notables such as

President Reagan, Jimmy Stewart, Gene Autry, Walt Disney, Leo Carrillo, and James Garner, to mention a few.

Before departing on this annual spring trek, club members head to Mission Santa Inés to receive a blessing for their horses. A dusty cloud appears on the horizon as close to six hundred riders approach the historic building. The roar of hooves grows louder and eventually fills the air. As the equestrians draw closer, spectators can hear the creaking of saddle leather accompanied by hearty laughter and voices of the Rancheros.

At the mission, large crowds wait in anticipation. Once the riders congregate, Padre Michael Mahony dispenses a traditional blessing, and soon the equines and their mounts depart, accompanied by cheers and good wishes from the audience. The Rancheros then head for the hills to indulge in a week filled with tests of horsemanship, rodeo skills, entertainment, and partying.

NATURE'S CHURCH
by Yvonne Hollenbeck

*Did you ever see the mountains that are covered up
   with snow, or watch a setting sun and see its purple
   afterglow?*

*Have you ever seen a newborn calf a-wobbling to its
   feet, and though it's only minutes old it knows just
   where to eat?*

*You can't climb upon a saddle horse and cross the
   prairie sod, or see an eagle on the wing and not
   believe in God.*

*A cowboy doesn't worship in a building made of stone,
   but worships with his Maker out with nature all alone.*

*His church is the great outdoors; the valley, heaven's gate,
   his favorite hymn's a coyote that is calling to its mate.*

*And he never does his tithing droppin' money in a hand,
   it's by being a good caretaker of the creatures and
   the land.*

*He makes his own communion while a choir of songbirds
   sings, cups his hands and drinks the fresh cold water
   from a spring.*

*With the budding of the springtime and with autumn's
   goldenrod, there's no better place to worship than to be
   out there with God.*

*So when you hear a meadowlark that's singing from his
   perch, he's inviting you to worship with him there at
   Nature's Church.*

Bénédiction des Chevaux, France

In France, one of the oldest equine blessings is the Bénédiction des Chevaux. Held for nineteen centuries, this blessing occurs in conjunction with La Festo Vierginenco in the region of Les Saintes Maries de la Mer, Camargue. However, across the realm, blessings happen throughout the year in association with other celebrations such as Easter, May Day, the feast day of St. Hubert, or during the Festival of the Shepherds.

One of the most popular blessing of the horses transpires at the fifth century Chapel of Notre Dame de la Salette (or Notre Dame de Trébillane). Each Easter Monday, nearly 500 horse riders come to the chapel to receive traditional blessings. Additional activities include bull races, games, riding exhibitions, and a street dance. Thousands attend this traditional ceremony established by Father Joseph Rey in 1958.

EQUINE BLESSING

Bless these beasts of burden.
May our steeds be swift of foot, calm of nature,
*   strong in body, and sound in mind.*
Give them the gift of a smooth gait.
Bestow them with exceptional health and long life.
Honor us with their presence, and make us
*   worthy stewards.*

✦ ✦ ✦

Palio della Contrada, Italy

Italians celebrate horses twice a year when Siena churches conduct an equine blessing in conjunction with the Palio horse race, a competitive race around Siena's main square. The Palio's origin dates back to August of 1310. The traditional race, a rivalry between Siena's *contrada* (districts), is short and concludes in less than two minutes. Once a pursuit through the streets of the town, the sprint now takes place on a crude track in Siena's Piazza del Campo of Siena, in the Tuscany region of Italy.

Official festivities begin three days prior to the race and include trial races, banquets, betting, and late-night carousing. Once selected, horses visit the church in the *contrada* for which they will run. Each receives a blessing such as, "Run, little horse, and return a winner." If a horse defecates during the individual blessing, cheers erupt from spectators, as it is considered good luck.

Preceding the race, residents don traditional dress and colors of their neighborhood. Neighbors march down lanes, wave flags, and keep in step to the tempo of musical instruments. The Palio, a banner dedicated to the Virgin Mary, leads equine competitors and jockeys to the starting line.

This important competition determines who gains the respect or scorn of rival Sienese. In July 1649, a second race was added, and although both races are of equal value, winners treasure the August event since it allows longer bragging rights.

HORSE BLESSING

Bless this horse.
We give thanks for this mount and ask that he be
*   fleet of foot.*
Keep his rider steady and focused.
May he run like the wind and carry us to glory,
*   so we may celebrate together until the next race.*

ENGELWEIHE, SWITZERLAND ❧ At Einsiedeln Monastery, near Zurich, Switzerland, another international equine celebration takes place. Founded in the tenth century, this monastery is one of the last that still breeds horses. Love of horses led to the creation of the Festival of the Engelweihe (Blessing of the Horses), an event attracting hundreds of horse riders.

Blessing of the Hounds

Although the name suggests a species-specific focus, the long-standing tradition of Blessing of the Hounds encompasses more than just hounds, since it includes all animals and humans involved in the hunt. The blessing practice dates back to the eighth century and to celebrations associated with St. Hubert. English hunters popularized this ritual and brought the custom to the American colonies in the seventeenth century.

Over a thousand people attended the 76th Anniversary of the Blessing of the Hounds at Grace Episcopal Church in Keswick, Virginia. The blessing tradition established by this Colonial church back in 1929 is extended to riders, horses, hounds, and even the fox (in absentia). During the anniversary, bagpipes played as Reverend Julie Norton, rector, prayed, "For the horses to be surefooted, the hounds to be swift and disciplined, and the foxes to be fleet of foot and elusive."

THANKSGIVING BLESSING
by Reverend Julie Norton

Almighty and everlasting God, who has given us all of life to enjoy, and the grace to return our thanksgivings to you:

Let your blessing be with all who participate in this Thanksgiving Day hunt.

Guide the riders safely through fields and woodlands, protect them from any accident, and bring them safely home.

May their horses be surefooted and strong, the hounds both swift and disciplined, and may the foxes be fleet of foot and elusive, running in their splendid glory to give the hounds a worthy chase.

Protect all creatures this Thanksgiving Day, and especially those who thank you through the exuberance of sport and activity, and please accept our enjoyment of this morning's hunt as an expression of gratitude for the wonders of Your creation. Amen.

Anglican Society for the Welfare of Animals, United Kingdom

Blessing services often include messages about animal welfare and human responsibility as stewards. One such group focused on those messages and based in England is the Anglican Society for the Welfare of Animals.

Their mission is to promote concern and awareness related to all aspects of God's animal creation within the Anglican Church and the wider Christian community. The group offers a wealth of printed resources to clergy and other interested parties.

Members believe it is a God-given responsibility for humans to care for other sentient beings who share this world. Constituents maintain that dominion is actually stewardship, and they encourage political and social involvement for animal protection. The Anglican Society actively encourages regular inclusion of animals in services and prayers to promote "gentle, kind, and generous" treatment of animals.

Part of their constitution states, ". . .God's ultimate purpose in creating this universe lies beyond it, in an eternal order of goodness and love, where his glory will be fully revealed in the blessedness of his creatures as they rejoice in the perfect communion with him and with one another."

To accomplish their goals, the group introduced Animal Welfare Sunday to parishes within the Church of England in 1972. These ongoing events promote animal welfare for all species and annually refresh the group's message in the minds of participants.

PRAYER FOR ANIMAL
WELFARE SUNDAY
by Linda J. Bodicoat

*Almighty God, maker of all living things, in whose
Fatherly wisdom we trust and depend. Enable us, by
the power of Your Holy Spirit, to recognize the works
of Your hand in all things.*

*We give thanks to You, O God, for the opportunity to
worship You on this special day, set aside as Animal
Welfare Sunday. We remember with joy and gratitude
all Your creatures, whose beauty and diversity enriches
our lives beyond measure.*

*We ask Your forgiveness for the many ways in which
animals are abused and exploited, through both
ignorance and greed, and we confess before You our
part in their suffering, acknowledging the times we
have remained silent, lacking the courage to speak out
in their defense.*

*Strengthen us in our resolve as we aspire to lead the
"simple" life of faith and obedience, free from all
earthly entrapments and material wealth, using earth's
resources wisely and thoughtfully, faithfully following
the example of Your servant St. Francis of Assisi.*

Help us, O Lord, as we endeavor to live in harmony
with all Your creatures, leaving only the footprints of
true discipleship upon this earth when we leave and
not the deep scars of greed and exploitation.

Encourage and inspire each one of us to grow in Your
likeness and to be remembered for our simplicity of
heart and generosity of spirit and for our "oneness"
with all creation.

Grant us, O merciful God, humble and contrite hearts
and a clear vision of Your purpose for us in Your
world, that we may become faithful stewards of
Your wonderful creation.

These things we ask in Jesus' name.
Amen.

✦ ✦ ✦

WORLD ANIMAL DAY 🌿 World Animal Day was first conceived at a 1931 meeting of ecologists in Florence, Italy. The day highlighted the plight of endangered species. However it wasn't until late 2003, when it was formally launched in the United Kingdom, that this October event became a worldwide celebration of animal life of all types.

PRAYER FOR CRITTER CONNECTION

Help us to learn from all our furry, finned, feathered,
*   and scaly neighbors.*
Let us rejoice in nature and all it offers.
Inspire us to recognize our similarities and differences.
Motivate us to respect one another as similar pieces in
*   the divine design.*
And allow us to discover our celestial connection.

PART TWO
Rites of Paws-sage:
Muzzle Tov!

Pet Mitzvahs

Pet Mitzvahs began in the 1980s as early harbingers of a trend now popular among pet owners of all faiths. Today pet mitzvah outfits, specialty Star of David snacks, appropriate collars, and themed pet tags for such events are common. Savvy shoppers may just order a complete "bark mitzvah" package. So, just what is so captivating about a terrier in a *tallit?* The answers vary as much as the people who throw such celebrations.

Rabbi Neil Comess-Daniels of Temple Beth Shir Shalom, a progressive Reform synagogue, held the shul's first community bark mitzvah around 1981. The affair continues to be held in the "barking" lot; participants receive a bark mitzvah certificate and, for a token fee, a commemorative photo.

In an interview with Orange County Jewish Life, Rabbi Neil said, "We do this event mostly as a lark, but the reality is that there is this beautiful underlying seriousness to it...it's a way to bring the community together."

Rachel Zuckerman, a reporter for the *Forward*, a Jewish newspaper, suggested that bark mitzvahs have become accepted rover rituals, offering ways to celebrate canine family members while raising money for synagogues and related charities.

BLESS THIS PET

May the One who has blessed our forefathers, foremothers, and their flocks, bless this pet.

We give praise and thanksgiving to the Almighty for all the good this animal brings to the world.

Holy One, keep him/her, sustain him/her, and make this animal a blessing to all he/she encounters.

✦ ✦ ✦

Equine Mitzvah

A small assembly of humans gathered together to celebrate the equine mitzvah of a gelding. Guests feasted on a variety of fish, held a candle-lighting ceremony, and listened to readings from a Hebrew prayer book. What started out as a silly ceremony became a memorable and heartwarming occasion for the owner and friends in attendance.

Held at his stable, the stately steed wore a prayer shawl and yarmulke. He also indulged in a sample of Manischewitz sacramental wine, which Norine Dresser said "cast an uncharacteristic calm over the steed."

Humans who were influential in the steed's life participated in the ceremony by stepping forward to light a candle on his cake. The handsome equine also received a multitude of gifts; some more appropriate for his human, others more to his liking, such as carrots, apples, sugar, and a bouquet of flowers that ended up as a snack after a solicitous sniff.

BLESSING OF A PET

*Sacred One, we are filled with gratitude for all the
    blessings bestowed upon us by You through (pet's name).
From the moment this animal arrived in our home, he/she
    has inspired joy in our lives and in those of others.
Surround this creature with devotion; continue to
    allow him/her to increase love and laughter for the
    individuals he/she encounters.
Keep him/her safe from harm. We ask that you give this
    animal strength in body, mind, and spirit.
Guide him/her to live in harmony within the household.
Permit this animal always to have loving, kind companion-
    ship for the rest of his/her life, and grant him/her
    a good old age filled with contentment and happiness.*

Barking Up the Wrong Tree?

Despite their popularity, debate over the appropriateness of pet mitzvahs continues. The *Miami Herald* reported that Rabbi Gary Glickstein of Temple Beth Sholom, a Reform synagogue, appreciates the different ways people find to express their Judaism. However, some rabbinical leaders remain offended over these "faux mitzvahs" and believe those who celebrate them are barking up the wrong tree.

Temple Beth Am, a Reform synagogue, has held pet blessings but not pet mitzvahs, Rabbi Terry Bookman said, "a bark mitzvah is a desecration of a sacred event" and is crossing the line, while Rabbi Ed Farber of Beth Torah, a Conservative congregation, said, "It is just distasteful."

Opinions continue to conflict, but these rover rituals are not meant to be a mockery of serious traditions. Instead they provide examples of how modern society integrates ancient traditions into contemporary lifestyles. Bark and meow mitzvahs are usually social events rather than coming-of-age ceremonies. In any case, variations on these life passage celebrations have gone beyond the walls of traditional religious centers and out into communities. They also get new people and their pets into spiritual centers.

TIMELESS BLESSING
May the lives of all those gathered here today be blessed with peace and harmony, and may we always act in a manner that reflects the radiance and virtues of our ancestors.

✦ ✦ ✦

Meow Mitzvah

When their fabulous feline hit adolescence, Sherry and David, a California couple, decided to celebrate with a large summer meow mitzvah. Nearly 100 people received invitations. The frivolity included gifts, food, dancing on the beach, and a rousing parody of two songs from *Fiddler on the Roof.*

So, what are appropriate gifts at a meow mitzvah? Cat bowls, teaser toys, a cat video with birds and bugs, and a variety of kitty snacks. Unfortunately, this picky pussycat hated wearing her traditional head covering and expressed her discontent through uncooperative, grumpy behavior. Miss Kitty distinctly stood out as the only one to express a complaint during the festivities.

Despite the lightheartedness of these events, pet parents share the desire to rejoice in the relationship with their precious companion animal. The underlying theme celebrates life with the critter and their deep connection. This is why established traditions get adapted to commemorate pets.

FELINE BLESSING

Dearest One, we give thanks for your many blessings
and gather together in thanksgiving to celebrate this cat.
Today we honor the passage of (cat's name) from kittenhood
into a fully fabulous feline.
His/her amusing antics have brought us joy and will
remain cherished memories throughout our life.
(Cat's name) reminds us to take time to enjoy the
simple pleasures of life, to relax, to play, to feast,
and to be affectionate without reserve.
As we celebrate, we ask that this animal live a long
comfortable life, enjoy security and love, and be
blessed for eternity in the manner of which he/she
has blessed all of us.

Bark Mitzvah

When a local entertainer mentioned he wanted to hold a party for his dog, several friends stepped forward to help. The party planners came up with a variety of ideas, but the winning proposal was a celebratory dinner theater production.

The night of the affair, Buddy, the guest of honor, donned a yarmulke and sported a fashionable bib patterned with the Star of David. Guests gathered in the dining area where an entertaining buffet awaited. Homemade crackers shaped like animal figures, fire hydrants, doghouses, and the Star of David bordered a paté molded into a caricature of a giant bone, which, interestingly enough, resembled wet dog food once guests finished with it. Other mouth-watering fare was served up in designer dog bowls. Gracing its own table was the blue and white star-shaped cake which read, "Muzzle Tov!"

At evening's end, guests departed with a variety of mementos of the occasion, blue skullcaps embroidered with Buddy's name and the celebration date, Star of David bandanas, and engraved pet tags for their own precious pets.

CANINE BLESSING

Thank you for joining us in celebration of (dog's name) life.
Join us now in a candle-lighting ceremony.
The purpose of this ritual is to recognize family and
friends who impact our lives and to allow them to
share their stories and praise.
The candle represents the divine light within each of us.
As your candle is lit, please share a positive story,
memory, or lesson learned from this pet.
Next light the candle of your neighbor on your left, who
will then repeat the tradition until the circle is complete.
May we all share the light this animal has brought to
our lives, and may that light bless him/her for all
of his/her days.

✦ ✦ ✦

Furry Fêtes

Although an occasional pooch planner might surface, pet owners usually arrange companion animal celebrations. Pet mitzvahs start out reasonable, but some pet enthusiasts spend thousands of dollars on the festivities.

Frivolity surrounding these events is standard, but pet mitzvahs also serve a more serious purpose as fundraisers for charities. Synagogues raise funds for favorite programs, while pet parents often request gifts be donated to local humane societies and shelters.

Is there a perfect time for a pet mitzvah? Not really. Pet parents commonly throw mitzvahs at six months, two years of age, or at thirteen months or years. Since neutering most often occurs at pet adolescence, shelters and other animal services might consider the merits of sponsoring an animal mitzvah to reward responsible ownership during pet maturation.

BLESSING FOR CREATION

Blessed are you, architect of the universe.
We sing praise for the fish of the sea, birds of the sky,
*   and wildlife of the woodlands.*
We thank you for the creatures whose beauty captivates
*   our eyes and whose symphonies fill our lives with*
*   enchantment.*
In this world, the exotic beasts fascinate and motivate
*   us to explore your creation.*
We marvel your vast palette of unusual and unique
*   organisms and thank you for all your living blessings.*

PART THREE
Muttrimony and
Other Pet Nuptials

L ike it or not, pet nuptials and related practices are on the rise.
For something exotic, travel to the island of Oahu. There, pets
enjoy a beach wedding complete with a minister officiant, photographer, and pet leis. No pet wedding license requirements exist, but
it's a good idea to check on quarantine issues before buying your tickets.

If you find yourself getting hot under the collar, consider the
possibility of taking these types of events less seriously. Remember,
pet weddings are not recognized by any government or church, so
they aren't legally binding. Even though pet weddings don't have any
official standing, they can be a lot of fun. For some people, the tradition resembles the neo-pagan ritual of hand-fasting, which
involves making a renewable contract for a specific amount of time.

Bonding Ceremony

In this ceremony, friends or families of pets braid ribbons together.
The colors can be significant to the duration of a breeding contract
or can celebrate a foster pet's temporary integration into a home.
Consider using white, blue, green, and orange ribbons to symbolize
the seasons. Such a composition can represent an annual commitment.

Friends and family form a ring around the ceremony platform for the exchange of declarations. If desired, guests can bring flowers, pet treats, or toys to decorate the altar. Pet parents might request that donations or gift certificates be given to homeless pets in shelters.

Surrounded by the sky and supported by the earth
    we gather today to celebrate this joining of two
    companion animals.
May your association be buoyant and take flight, soar
    to great heights, and be filled with positive movement
    and change.
May your bond be solid and grow deep roots so you
    experience a firm foundation and nourishing liaison.

The braided ribbons may be symbolically looped in a figure eight or intertwined loosely around the necks of the pets. Alternatively, collars may be exchanged and placed on the animals by the pet parents.

Walk the path of this bonding ceremony in peace,
    harmony, and joy.
Be filled with vitality, passion, and light.
Like the rays of the sun, may your love melt any harsh
    winters of life.
May your elation banish any sorrows.
Go now, and may the vitality in your veins shine through
    you and light up the lives of those around you.

Pet Weddings, Texas

Minister Lynn Turner of Deer Park, Texas, performs pet weddings and other animal-related services in addition to her normal roles as a minister. She first began conducting animal events after a request by Special Pals, a local animal rescue group.

Reverend Turner often officiates over cat ceremonies. She said when it was time to exchange kisses at the end of one memorable ceremony, the bride slapped the groom! This was not the first time something like this happened; in the pet nuptial world, holy muttrimony is much easier than a cat connection.

Reverend Turner's pet wedding ceremonies usually last about thirty minutes. They begin with a traditional bridal march processional, end with a recessional, and are followed by a reception. She even uses unique "Bow Wow Vows" or "Meow Vows" for services.

When asked for tips, Reverend Turner said, "Dogs and cats don't do well together in mixed ceremonies." Still, she performs group weddings successfully despite feline and canine misgivings.

This critter-friendly clergywoman gives the following suggestions to people who want to create a successful pet ceremony: Retain a sense of humor; use kitty and doggie treats to keep the attention of pet participants; register the bride and groom at local pet establishments; and—as an extra-nice touch—pre-train critters for vocal vows of commitment.

Pet Vows

Make up pet vows or construct a version closely parallel to traditional wedding vows. The exchange of collar practice is popular between different ministers performing pet weddings, but feel free to create a unique ceremony!

Dear friends and family, we are joyfully gathered today as witnesses to a blessed union of two special critters. Do you (male pet) take (female pet) to be your loving, playful, and faithful companion from this day forward? Will you promise to share this relationship through the remaining seasons of this year/life and to romp together in all weather, fair or foul? Will you promise to be obedient, to share your bowls, beds, and toys? Do you pledge your unconditional love, and promise to nuzzle and cuddle in good times as well as in bad? Is it your intent to refrain from biting when a simple growl will do? Do you agree to share your lives with many friends and family members? Will you create new memories of a life together and overlook your personal histories?"

Rhinestone, gold, or silver collars are now exchanged with help from human attendants:

> *Do you (male pet) and (female pet) exchange and wear these collars as symbols of your love and commitment, promise to honor your vows, remain loyal companions, and always strive to do your best?*
> *I hereby pronounce you joyful animal companions!*

✦ ✦ ✦

Hollywood Hounds. California

Drive down Sunset Boulevard to discover Hollywood Hounds. For those with a couple of thousand to spend, contact this center for the ultimate in pet nuptials. The eclectic facility provides a unique location complete with a gazebo. Guests are transported to and from the event in a limo. Amenities include a red carpet, musicians, floral arrangements, grooming for the bride and groom, mineral water, champagne, a cake for humans, another for canines, and necessary attire for the happy couple.

So, is there a need for a prenuptial agreement? In some arrangements, families make contracts for offspring, but many encourage others to consider a pre-nip-tual, to take the bite out of things, so to speak.

Starlight Connection

Gather together under the starlit skies for this blending ceremony.

Under this garland of stars we give quiet witness to
the blending of these beloved pets and their families.
May the wind carry these promises upward into the
celestial concourse for all to hear.
We ask a blessing on these creatures and ask that they
be protected throughout their union.
May the bonds between them be strong and may the
winds of change be gentle.
May their love spark great things in the lives of
their people.
May their affectionate natures catalyze deep and rich
relationships with all those they encounter.
May they always receive strong, consistent support from
their humans.
May their light shine eternally.

Families take two candles (representing the two family units) and light one large votive (representing their friendship and pet bonds). Officiant leads:

These candles represent the beacon of love brought to these families by their pets.

May they always see that light and be guided by its luminosity.

May their love for these pets burn with a steady flame and lead them down the path of compassion and understanding.

Should that flame flicker, they promise to guard and shield it.

We ask that this candle remind us all to aspire to love unconditionally and to allow a soft glow to emanate from our heart to others.

May this union bring to your families the power of commitment, inspiration from above, emotional growth, deep sentiment, light, and vitality.

Go in peace.

✦ ✦ ✦

Wild Kingdom of Weddings

If pet weddings seem a bit too much, consider pet participation in human nuptials. Sound silly? Don't dismiss the notion of a mutt-of-honor or similar pet participation. Sheep dog Winston escorted his pop diva mistress, Gwen Stefani, down the aisle. Comedian and film star Adam Sandler asked his dog Meatball to serve as "Best Bulldog" at his wedding. Even Martha Stewart tackled the topic, giving cutting-edge tips in her magazine, *Martha Stewart Living*, about how to involve pets in ceremonies successfully.

Birds, cats, dogs, llamas, elephants, and other animals participate in creative ceremonies in a variety of ways. Examples include couples arriving on horseback or small pets, such as ferrets or rabbits, carried in baskets by bridesmaids.

Cats and birds do better left at home, but include them in photos placed near the guest book. Some critters attend ceremonies housed in appropriately decorated carriers placed behind the officiant. Believe it or not, parrots have flown down the aisle to deliver rings (fake) to the bride and groom. Canine attendants walk the wedding pathway partnered with handlers while human attendants transport cats or pocket pets.

Creature Celebration

Gather a brass bell, sea salt, water, rose petals, incense (frankincense, sandalwood, sage, or sweet grass), a tree branch, blessed water, two candles, rose oil or rose water, a rose crystal rod, and two collars/leashes.

Create a circle for this ceremony. Erect the main altar or platform in the north or center. Have the guests stand within the circumference of the circle while pets and family stand in the center before the altar.

To begin, ring a bell four times for each direction (North, South, East, West). Consecrate the circle with salt, water, and incense. Ring the bell three times.

 *Dear Heavenly Father, Divine Mother, Beloved*
Spirit everywhere present, we ask for your blessing
and protection.
We gather together in love and light to bless these pets.
May they enjoy health, joy, love, and stability.

Sprinkle salt before them.

> *Bless these animals of the earth with all the necessities*
> *of life.*

Light the altar candles and smudge the animals with incense.

> *Bless these pets and encircle them with light.*
> *Surround them in the warmth of love.*

Sprinkle water over the pets with a tree branch.

> *Bless these creatures and immerse them in deep affection.*

Anoint the pets' foreheads with rose water or rose oil.

> *Bless these beasts so each exhale envelops them with*
> *kindness.*

Collars are exchanged and leashes loosely entwined.

*These collars and leashes represent the ties between
the two animals/families.
The binding is loose because it is voluntary and
without restriction.
May you choose this union and enjoy its blessings.*

Sprinkle rose petals clockwise around the animals.

*Let the scent of these petals permeate the air so that
sweetness always surrounds you.
May the floral splendor represented here symbolize
the richness that will color your lives.
Go now and forever remain encircled by love until
the end of your days.*

Close the ceremony by ringing the bell three times.

PART FOUR

Pet Parties:
A Pawsitive Fur-nomenon

Looking to hold a purr-fect affair? Schedule a pet party. The selection is far from tame because choices come from a variety of furry festivities sparked by annual events, holidays, or special occasions. Fund-raising events can range from an elaborate New Year's Eve Fur Ball or a Canine Cotillion to a Bark and Art cocktail party or a Whine and Cheese reception.

What to serve? Pet-savvy attendants know the only drink for thirsty pets is water. For the ulti-mutt in bottled water, sample the purified water available in a variety of flavors from the K9 Water Company. Serve it in upscale martini-style pet bowls labeled, "Mutt-ini" or "Cosmo-paw-itan" to add a touch of class.

Get human party animals to drool over wines with names such as Pee-No Noir, Chateau La Paws or Canine Cabernet. State-of-the-arf wines are available from the Dog House,® a division of Kendall Jackson Wine Estates. Chief dog officer, Robbie, knows about pedigrees, making no bones over the fact that canines put the best connoisseurs to shame. So, the Dog House® motto confirms, "dog nose best." The innovative label also donates a portion of the proceeds from each bottle to Guide Dogs for the Blind.

Both pet parents and animal businesses enjoy yappy hours, meow mixers, puppy socials, and Yowl-O-Ween. Let the mind run wild to create unique merrymaking around naming ceremonies, teething awards, obedience graduation, fund-raisers, adoption anniversaries, special pet days, birthdays, puppy or kitten showers, and other seasonal galas.

For instance, create a seasonal splash by holding a pet fashion show in conjunction with fashion week. Boutiques and specialty pet centers celebrate nationally televised pet competitions with a Barkfast at Tiffany's party and similar galas.

Don't forget events such as spring picnics, parades, and beastly beauty contests—and be sure to offer pet photo opportunities with the Easter Bunny and Santa Paws. It is fun and rewarding to find festive themes coinciding with other national holidays and events.

Whether plans dictate a simple or complex event, the rule of thumb is to make it fun, fun, fun! For added adventure hire a pet party planner, or to avoid the hassle altogether, contract a location from an established specialist. The amount spent depends on just how elaborate the festivities get.

Professional parties start at under a hundred dollars and can escalate up into the thousands. Most facilities offer a package price for a set number of human and animal guests. Popular pooch parties include games, snacks, goodie bags, and a cake. Think about arranging sophisticated doggie dinners, equine extravaganzas, feline fêtes, or wild social events.

For those with a creative spirit, plan a unique extravaganza with a human and pet friendly menu. The fun begins during planning and preparation but doesn't stop there. Arrange to finish preparations early so the only concern is when to join in the merriment.

Dog Day Afternoon

For her first bash, Gina provided a meal palatable to everyone. The menu included meatloaf enhanced by a mashed potato topping serving as the "cake." She used ketchup to inscribe, "Happy Corky Day" across the concoction. In addition, Gina provided a tossed salad and drinks for humans. The popular cartoon dog, Blue, of Blue's Clues™ adorned the invitations, hats, plates, cups, tablecloth, and doggie bags.

When guests arrived, each received a hat and a sack stuffed with doggie treats, so that every canine guest, present or not, got something. The entire party, infused with laughter, lasted two hours. Everyone sang an off-key rendition of "Happy Corky Day" to the guest of honor, followed by gift opening.

After a dog nap, guests took a lakeside jaunt to accommodate the party pooch of honor. His favorite activity of romping in water concluded the day. Needless to say, Corky was one happy, tired canine at day's end. The memory continues to put smiles on the faces of everyone who attended.

HAPPY PET DAY SONG
Happy (pet's name) day to you,
Happy (pet's name) day to you,
Happy (pet's name) day, we love you,
Happy (pet's name) day to you!

✦ ✦ ✦

Real Party Animals

Pet parties and similar trends began gaining popularity in the 1990s. Today pet accessory mail order catalogs include party favors, and pet bakeries ship cakes around the United States. Even greeting card companies supply distinctive salutations for companion animal birthdays and a variety of other holidays and celebrations.

Puppy socials, yappy hours, meow mixers, and Howl-o-Ween parties are now the rage. Sophisti-cats and cos-mutt-politans turn up in canine couture and wearing trendy feline fashions. Pets looking for a good time find new pals with similar interests at these perfect gatherings; structured socials allow people to meet and snack along with pets. Usually hosted by humane societies, animal training facilities, and upscale pet bakeries, these fun events satisfy both humans and animals.

PRIMITIVE PARTIERS ❧ Pups love to party! Brenda, an innovative animal trainer in California, held puppy socials regularly in a large, fenced park. New arrivals met everyone else in controlled conditions, first through the fence. Once integrated into the group, pups learned to return to owners despite heavy distraction (playing with other dogs), received schooling in mutt manners, got great exercise, and benefited from optimal mental stimulation.

Brenda said, "Puppy socials are fabulous fun. Everyone gets to learn about pet behavior in a fun and painless manner. Pups gain valuable social skills in addition to wearing themselves out so their parents enjoy a quiet afternoon!"

PUPPY PRAYER

We give thanks for this puppy.
Help restore our fortitude by uplifting us and gifting
*   us with uninterrupted sleep.*
Assist us so we do not give in to puppy protests.
Guard our possessions from this canine chewer and
*   protect our floors from this house-soiling hound.*
Aid us in surviving the perils of rearing this young
*   doggie delinquent.*
We ask for an increase in mutt manners.
Help us recognize the cherished canine we brought home.
Give us a new perspective in the morning and let us
*   remember that the precious pup that first captured*
*   our hearts is still there—somewhere.*

Meow Mixers

Finicky felines and other animals pose greater difficulties for party planners. Although just as much fun, most other critters lack animal pals when compared to canines. However, don't get discouraged, since many enjoy playing games, receiving new toys, or reveling in special attention from humans.

Small, intimate meow mixers top the list of popular feline festivities. Popular in community rooms of humane societies, most consist of potential adopters and supporters visiting animals already acclimated to each other. Contrary to popular belief, cats are social creatures. Fabulous felines also top the list as the number one urban pet of choice, so anticipate more adventures of the feline kind in the near future.

Festivities for felines may have been overlooked by the masses, but a few feline fanatics celebrate their kitties in innovative ways. In the San Bernardino mountain communities, quite a few businesses have real animals as supervisors. Locals and visitors love the opportunity to socialize with pets while they shop. A unique cat with a ton of canine and feline friends, Sasha was a Himalayan beauty who enjoyed going back and forth to work with her human handmaiden, Beth. The small bookstore clientele loved Sasha, and many customers dropped by solely to visit the kitty queen. As the anniversary of the business fast approached, Beth pondered providing a meow mixer instead of a traditional party. Sasha, the center of attention, benefited from the decision. Not only did local patrons attend bearing a multitude of presents for the pussycat, but a variety of community cat lovers showed up as well.

KITTEN PRAYER

We give thanks for this kitten.

*Teach restraint to our miniature pouncing puma so
we can again enjoy a continuous night of sleep.*

Guard our sofa and curtains from clawing capers.

*Aid us in surviving the perils faced rearing this young
felonious feline.*

*Keep our dress clothes and legs safe from the climbing
antics of our tiny pocket panther.*

*Spare our bare toes by helping us to avoid early morning
hairball discoveries.*

*Ease our bonds of servitude to this kitty queen/cat
conqueror so that we instead become valued staff
members.*

*Let this crazy kitten evolve into a fabulous feline—
and let that happen soon!*

✦ ✦ ✦

Yappy Hours

The latest happenings on the urban interspecies social scene include
yappy hours. These critter collectives originated from attempts to
meet the social needs of pet facility supporters and animals.

Many innovative shelters hold pooch parties regularly. At one
such facility, dogs, owners, and shelter animals meet adjacent to their
shelter in a fenced dog park. Fees vary according to the theme or

season but include both a dog and human snack menu. People enjoy the outing, dogs romp, and canines get adopted.

Participants must obey "paw and order" guidelines at regularly scheduled sessions. Weekly or monthly gatherings may request donations, while annual fund-raisers sell tickets to events that include yappetizers, whining, and dining.

During the Westminster Dog Show, local hotels provide yappy hours scheduled to tie into the weeklong blitz of art auctions, awards banquets, canine couture fashion shows, and similar activities. Other hotels and inns use interspecies events creatively throughout the year. In San Francisco, California, a lodge invites singles to mingle alongside animal lovers on Valentine's Day. The mixer also benefits a local animal rescue group.

Yappy hours often follow a theme, sometimes planned and sometimes spontaneous. In Portland, Maine, specific-breed lovers started showing up at doggie diva Franny Murphy's monthly gathering. The first same-breed congregation may have appeared to be spontaneous, but breed enthusiasts actually planned the massive onslaught. A creative shelter in Jefferson, Louisiana, assigns monthly topics. The "No Sex in the City" focused on the battle against pet overpopulation, while "Hobo Hounds" centered on homelessness.

SMOOTH SAILING PRAYER

As we navigate into a new year with this pet
May the wind fill our sails for smooth sailing
May the sun warm our hearts and light our path
And as we embark on each new adventure, may
we experience joy, peace, and restoration.

✦ ✦ ✦

CRUISING CANINE 🐾 Debbie began attending dog parks regularly just as soon as Shasta arrived. As a result, the two made tons of friends. When Shasta's first birthday loomed on the horizon, Debbie decided on a canine cruise. The invitations read, "Sail into Shasta's new year on a canine cruiser. Coastal tour begins at the Mutt Marina...Dress in dog-gone fancy duds and join the party animals. Prompt pups only! Bring towels, toys, swimsuits, and sunscreen."

Dogs and owners turned out dressed in sailor suits and sporting fashionable goggles, visors, and themed collars and leashes. The boat stayed moored at the dock while dogs played in open cabin quarters and accompanied owners during deck-top strolls.

Yappetizers included gourmutt dog food and biscuits. Humans indulged in "Dog Perignon," salmon, caviar, and other delectables. A string quartet played during afternoon tea and then everyone disembarked for a shoreline splash. Talk about the ulti-mutt celebration!

Furry Festivities

During Christmas, Hanukkah, and Yule, attract feathered friends and even some furry visitors through innovative holiday creations. Animal-loving homes provide outdoor holiday decor for local avian clans by crafting bird-friendly trees filled with seed sprays, thistle-net balls, bird-toy decorations, and clever fresh fruit garlands.

For barnyard buddies, construct wreaths of hay adorned with carrots, apples, and an assortment of goodies. Don't forget to arrange additional time for winter pampering during inclement weather. Clean coats and protective measures for tenderfeet help keep critters dry and warm when they need it most.

Faux Paws?

A passionate discourse about the appropriateness of pets in holiday greeting cards ensued on a popular morning television show. Perhaps the commentators missed estimates concerning pet holidays. The American Pet Association collects fun facts about the status of pet households. During the last survey, the group reported holiday purchases exceeded 31 million for pooch presents and surpassed 39 million for cat offerings. Add those admired animals to holiday cards and gift lists!

To meet those demands, Santa Paws photo opportunities and pet presents flood aisles of specialty stores. So, take advantage of the multitude of unique furry festivities in local businesses since more and more include pets of all types.

PET PRAYER
Furry friends with loving hearts
Nestled at our feet
Warm our hearts and hearths.
We ask that they be eternally blessed
May they always be kept safe
Have a comfortable place to sleep and
Receive nourishment and loving care for
as long as they shall live.

✦ ✦ ✦

Jungle of Pet Pageants and Critter Contests

Include holiday hounds and festive felines during your Valentine's Day celebrations, but lean toward safe choices by bestowing some beastly bling or fashion accessory on the pet. Pet lovers purchase reflective ID hearts to protect a pet and express deep sentiments. Many even arrange a pet picnic on the beach, at a park, or pawtisserie. Perhaps the pampered pooch or puss needs a spa day. If a fund-raiser is in order, don't forget to set up a kissing booth and staff it with furry faces!

Pet pageants increase annually. Haute dogs gather every year to participate in beastly bonnet competitions, pet parades, and furry float competitions for Easter and May Day. So, get dramatic duds to celebrate flower power, enroll in a local egg hunt, or let pets rummage at home for hidden plastic eggs stuffed with favorite dog or kitty treats.

Join the Mystic Krewe of Barkus in Saint Louis, Missouri, as they celebrate Mardi Gras, Carnival style. Enrollment is open to most pups. Past themes of the party include "Jurassic Bark," "Lifestyles of the Bitch and Famous," "Tails from the Crypt," and the "Wizard of Paws."

Beauty contests or other affairs occur in conjunction with Mother's Day. Others are spawned as parodies of human contests. For the past 32 years hermit crabs have clawed to win the "Cucumber Cup" at the annual Miss Crustacean contest in Ocean City, New Jersey. Scandal erupted in area tabloids one year when experts revealed a male hermit crab contestant had accepted the coveted award. However, founder Mark Soifer quickly dismissed the drama since the contest does not discriminate by gender. To provide something for everyone, the revelry also includes wrestling contests between opponents such as Hogan Hermit or Crabilla Monsoon.

Seasonal favorites vary. On Father's Day enter the pooch and pop in a "hairiest dog and dad" competition, or stump judges in a "who's your daddy" contest. In San Pedro, California, both pets and humans join in the fall Lobster Festival festivities. Canines celebrate dressed as sea creatures in competition for the coveted "Lobster Dog" title. Later in the year, travel to Cincinnati, Ohio, to see dogs participate in an annual "Reindog Parade."

Feasting occurs during many other holidays, such as St. Patrick's Day, the Fourth of July, and Thanksgiving. Clever Irish breed clubs throw "Kiss me, I'm Irish" parties to raise money. Others dress pets in cheerful attire themed for the particular day and include critters in humane holiday gatherings.

Unfortunately, feasting fiestas pose great threats to pets who overeat or consume the wrong types of food or drink. To avoid problems, bake specialty treats appropriate for pets, and keep critters out of harm's way through prevention and supervision. Panicky pets do best safely stowed away in a boarding facility during fireworks displays.

PRAYER FOR A PEACEABLE KINGDOM

As we gather today in celebration,
We ask for a peaceable kingdom.
May peace permeate this event so all remain safe.
Fill our hearts with joy and make this joyful day
*   memorable for all who attend.*

Howl-o-Ween

Howl-o-Ween parties get really wild. Parties and parades just touch the tip of the iceberg, according to the American Pet Products and Manufacturers Association. The group estimates that over 3.7 million dog owners purchase gifts or costumes for pets specifically for Halloween festivities.

For the human guests, serve hors d'oeuvres such as yappy meals (a hamburger, French fries, and a toy) or "hallowieners" (hot dogs). Dish up treats specially designed for pets, to avoid upset stomachs. Chocolate, candy, and rich foods can harm or even kill pets. Avoid caffeine and alcohol. Make a big splash by allowing the canine culture to bob for hot dogs. Schedule this in conjunction with warm weather and provide towels. Otherwise substitute pooch popcorn or pup-sicles instead.

Creative costumes at boo bashes may include a dog dressed as a taxicab or as a Hawaiian tourist. Fairy princess, angel, and Western character costumes proved most popular at the second annual Halloween Party at Doodledings Dog Bakery and Boutique in Burlingame, Alabama.

Small dog costume designer Alexandra Camarillo coordinates costumes with her pet Chihuahua, Lola. Once the two stepped out as an angel and devil. Recently the pair debuted as Dorothy and the Wicked Witch from the *Wizard of Oz*. Lola, outfitted in a replica dress, also sported a pigtailed doll wig and ruby paw slippers. She charmed everyone during her trick-or-treating at pet stores.

Because not everyone is as gifted as designer Camarillo, Rubie's Costumes of New York, the world's largest costume manufacturer, began offering pet costumes seven years ago. Then, pet parents selected from six costume choices. Today the collection exceeds forty different designs—a growth rate of 60 percent. Nowadays the pet costume market accounts for 6 percent of total costume sales, which translates into about 40 million dollars.

Howard Beige, executive vice-president, says the top commercial canine costumes include *Star Wars*® characters, Yoda and Darth Vader, followed closely by Super Dog. Other popular costumes include Scooby Doo,® Looney Tunes® characters, and skeletal dog Scraps, from the *Corpse Bride*.™

Want to just horse around? Join Halloween with Horses in Parker, Colorado, for a day filled with unique happenings. In addition to costume contests, experience the stable of terror, preview a puppet show, enter the trick-or-treat barn bash, ride ponies, or visit a pumpkin patch.

Posh Pet Costume Safety Tips

- Make sure costumes and masks do not restrict vision or breathing.
- If the pet is unwilling or uncomfortable, don't force him or her to dress up or wear a costume.
- Acclimate the pet to wearing a costume in advance of the parade or party.
- Keep pets under close watch so they don't get spooked by spooks.

AUTUMN ANIMAL BLESSING

*On this day let us remember our ancestors and all the
    animals who have graced our lives.*
We are thankful for the blessings animals bring.
*We are thankful for the smiles, comfort, and gifts
    bestowed upon us by all creatures.*
Let us celebrate the harvest and abundance of this time.
*During the festivities we ask for compassion, protection,
    and guidance.*
*Keep watch over us, guide us, and bestow blessings on
    everyone we meet, today and always.*

Groundhog Gala

Groundhog Day occurs halfway between the winter solstice and
spring equinox. In the United States, wild and wacky groundhog
"weathermen" stick their necks out to make weather predictions
early in the year. Real animals, these groundhogs "forecast" the end of
winter or beginning of spring in an old tradition linked to Candlemas.
The most famous weather-predicting groundhog is Punxsutawney Phil,
although unconfirmed rumors indicate that Connecticut Chuckles
launched a campaign to usurp him.

    Fans and residents in Punxsutawney, Pennsylvania, celebrate
annually. Since 1887 Phil has made his prediction at Gobblers
Knoll, where thousands turn out to watch. Phil's notoriety earns him
an entourage of staff members. In addition to his "inner circle," an

official scribe, media liaison, and escorts for his meeting with White House dignitaries form the personnel surrounding him.

CANDLEMAS DAY (Scotland, circa 1898)
If Candlemas Day be dry and fair,
The half of the winter's to come and mair.
If Candlemas Day be wet and foul,
The half of the winter is gone at Yule (Christmas).

✦ ✦ ✦

CANDLEMAS DAY (United States, circa 1898)
On Candlemas Day the bear, badger, or woodchuck
comes out to see his shadow at noon: if he does not
see it, he remains out; but if he does see it, he goes
back to his hole for six weeks, and cold weather
continues for six weeks longer.

✦ ✦ ✦

Feathering the Nest
Many pet parents now register with local pet stores or boutiques prior to parties. Pet households need a variety of items before getting a new critter, and with a registry, guests won't ponder over what is needed. Some common necessities include bowls, collars, leashes, pet carriers, pet strollers, toys, chew items, climbing aids, toileting and

clean-up products, furniture-chewing deterrents, snacks, breed or obedience books, and training videos. Also ask for recommendations or gift certificates for services such as grooming, veterinary medical care, day care, training, pet sitting, or boarding. Don't forget seatbelts, beds, pet gates, play pens, and cat trees.

BLESSING FOR NEW BIRTH

Great Artist, we pray for these new arrivals and praise
you for these new beings.

Allow these furry gifts to grow into healthy, magnificent
creatures.

May they always be kept in friendly company and find
loving homes.

Spare them from the dangers of vehicles, diseases, parasites,
and other threats.

Awaken their senses and let them gladden the hearts of
all those they meet.

Let them teach unconditional love and how to live in
the moment.

Through their heightened senses, allow us to awaken to
the wonder of discovery.

Via their example of acceptance, let them edify tolerance.
We thank you for this gift of life before us now and
for the many blessings to come by affiliation with
your creations.

Showering Species

In advance of the birth of a litter, or prior to bringing an adopted pet home, celebrate the occasion with friends and family by holding a pet shower. It is a great time to receive pet essentials and glean necessary tips in advance of the initiation (or return) to pet parenthood. Send invitations to pet-friendly pals asking for their best tips and recipes for the expected addition.

PRAYER FOR PET SELECTION

Great Spirit everywhere present, we ask for your help and assistance.

Guide us on our quest to find the perfect pet for this home/family.

Help us find the right animal, revealing the best match with a clear sign.

We ask that the integration be smooth, joyful, and uplifting for all involved.

Assist us in finding humane teachers and compassionate pet professionals to help us care for this pet, and make our lifetime together a sacred union.

Nom de Plume

Lynn lives at the edge of the national forest with a dozen dogs. Very irresponsible people think animals can survive on their own, and such people abandon these poor creatures in the wilderness. Some of these abandoned animals eventually arrive on Lynn's doorstep, emaciated from hunger, lacking trust in humans.

Despite hardships, the devastated dogs eventually come around. Lynn has developed a unique naming ceremony to help with integration. She says, "I believe the dog needs a new name and should participate in the selection of it. So, I recite the alphabet, watching to see what letter the dog responds to. After that, I make up a variety of names and the one the dog seems to like is the one the dog gets."

Make pet naming, adoption ceremonies, and birth or arrival celebrations unique. The decision to add a new animal to the home is both a serious and joyous occasion. Adding a new pet impacts family members, so plan the adoption of an animal with great forethought and care.

PRAYER FOR A NEW PET

*Heavenly Dweller, we thank you for creating this lovely
    animal and placing him/her in our hands.
May we be blessed as his/her caretakers, and may this
    household be filled with joy.
Bless our relationship with this pet.
Guide us in our care for this creature.
May this bond uplift our family as long as we live together.
We give thanks for the love and glory manifested through
    all creation.*

✦ ✦ ✦

Beastly Travelers

According to the Travel Industry Association of America, some
29.1 million Americans have traveled with a pet in the past three
years. The burgeoning group of beastly travelers ride fashionably in
their own cushy carriers or wheeled travel crates, or sit pretty (and
safely) outfitted in their own specialty seatbelts and other travel
accessories. Pet passports, unique airline travel bonuses, and pet-
oriented hotel programs make traveling with pets easier.

The pet-traveling trend increases during the summer, when more
families travel on vacation. Estimates indicate that of all pet travelers,
78 percent are canines. Felines take second place at 15 percent; the
remaining 7 percent includes birds, ferrets, and fish. Vehicular travel
by auto or truck is the primary mode of transportation, topping the

list at 76 percent. Other popular modes of transport include expeditions via recreational vehicles (10 percent) airline travel (6 percent) and excursions by train, rental vehicle, or motor coach (8 percent).

PRAYER FOR PET TRAVEL

As our pets embark on this journey we ask that they be
surrounded by the light of protection.

Keep them safe during this excursion and let them reach
their destination safely.

We ask that their means of transportation be surrounded
by a protective shield.

Guard our pets throughout their travels and keep them
calm, happy, and secure.

✦ ✦ ✦

Pets Gone Astray

Millions of lost animals turn up in shelters around the United States every year. Even with the best precautions, animals can escape through an open door, unscreened window, unlatched gate, dropped leash, or by unexpectedly bolting during travel, sometimes in fearful response to thunder or other noise.

Experts agree that the best way to avoid lost pets is to make sure animals always wear collars with identification tags on them. In addition, nationally registered microchip implants or tattoos can help return pets home safely.

PRAYER FOR LOST ANIMAL

Help us in our time of distress.

Guide our wayward animal back to our arms quickly.

Keep (name of pet) safe and lead him/her to find the
way home.

If this is not possible, land our precious pet in the care
of humane humans.

Please bestow blessings upon our beloved furry family
member and give us peace.

We pray for comfort, assistance, and guidance.

✦ ✦ ✦

When Disaster Strikes

Hurricane Katrina victims lost nearly everything: their homes, jobs, and possessions. What really broke hearts, however, was the loss of family pets. A year after the hurricane only 15 percent of the lost animals had been reunited with their families. Many other disaster survivors can reveal similar experiences of fires, floods, earthquakes, or man-made catastrophes. The lesson? Always have an emergency pet-supply kit on hand and include your animals in any evacuation plans.

The demographics of pet owners have created a burgeoning industry dedicated to pet rescue and care. Municipal, state, and national governments now realize that emergency management agencies must address pet needs during a crisis. On a national level, the

Pets Evacuation and Transportation Standards Act passed in both the House of Representatives and also in the Senate. Now assigned to committee, this indicates the importance of addressing pet and pet-owner needs during a crisis.

PRAYER FOR DISASTER RECOVERY

*We call out to you, God, and ask for intercession on
    behalf of the animals.*

Help these victims of disaster.

*Give them safe harbor, provide them with nourishment,
    and quench their thirst.*

*Lead lost pets into kind hands and unite them with
    their families.*

*Supply wild creatures with new homes and abundant
    resources.*

*We pray for speedy recovery of all those affected by this
    catastrophe.*

Let peace and healing fill the area.

*And bless those called upon to assist during this time
    of tragedy.*

One Sick Puppy: Illness or Injury

Veterinary Pet Insurance Company (VPI) reported spikes in claims during summer months. VPI believes this is due to increased activity outdoors. Long life spans and advances in the complexity of veterinary medical care have changed pet health-care practices. Like medical doctors, veterinarians now specialize in specific areas, such as oncology.

In the past, animals visited the veterinarian for an annual checkup, shots, or emergency care. Today preventative veterinary care includes bi-annual visits, dental care, and a variety of specialty services. In addition, lifestyle diets and alternative practices are gaining popularity.

PET HEALING PRAYER

Divine Physician, send healing energy to (pet's name).
Remove any pain or suffering.
If it is for the highest good, take away his/her malady.
Restore this creature to optimal health.
Keep (pet's name) under watch and surround him/her
    with love.

Compassionate Critter Care

The life span of pets has increased in response to veterinary care services. Age-related pet challenges and illnesses can now be treated with interventions, including hip replacements, chemotherapy, transplants, and neurosurgery. New advances in veterinary medicine began in the mid 1980s and continue unabated. One of the newest services in the field of pet medicine is pet hospice.

Following the model of compassionate palliative care for humans, pet hospice care focuses on giving pets a safe, intimate end-of-life experience at home. It also teaches the family how to cope with the loss of a pet.

According to Dr. Cheryl Scott, a veterinarian hospice provider in California since 1998, many animals in hospice care die peacefully during sleep. Dr. Scott sees hospice as promoting quality of existence at life's end. She advises euthanasia when appropriate.

Hospice care emphasizes quality of life, and patients receive symptom relief, physical affection, favorite food treats, and additional family time. The American Association of Human-Animal Bond Veterinarians, formed in 1993, promotes veterinary hospice in anticipation of specialty board certification some day. Veterinary hospice care guidelines received approval from the American Veterinary Medical Association in 2001, so certification may eventually become a reality.

Coming to terms with the inevitable loss of a pet can be difficult. In most cases, pet owners need to make decisions regarding a pet's quality of life and whether euthanasia is a responsible choice.

These decisions are usually made with professional guidance from a veterinarian.

According to Kathryn D. Marocchino, founder of The Nikki Hospice Foundation for Pets, "It is vital to help clients say good-bye to pets in their own way, to embrace their right to make personal and private choices for the pet's final days, and to offer veterinary care to maximize the quality of life for those terminally ill or dying pets."

PRAYER FOR PET RECOVERY
Divine Doctor, if it is your will, restore the health and strength of this animal.

✦ ✦ ✦

Trusting Tails

An estimated 66 percent of Americans die without a will in place. Of those who do prepare a will, only 12–15 percent remember to include provisions for future care of their pets. Estimates indicate that at least 500,000 pets are euthanized annually in the United States due to disability or death of their human caregivers. So it is important for pet owners to plan for the long-term care of their critters, in case the pets outlive them.

In 1923 the Kentucky Supreme Court was the first to address the issue of companion-animal care when it upheld a trust bequest to a pet. *USA Today* reported that pet-care trusts are currently honored in about half the states across the United States. Pet trusts help clarify wills and assign pet caretakers.

Pet owners can make provisions in their estate plans for the perpetual care of pets through an attorney or a pet trust business. The legal document mandates how pet custodians will operate and covers activities from daily diet, exercise, and veterinary care to burial specifications. But pet-care trusts are not the only option.

Consider a variety of alternatives when planning for pets. Parrots in Arizona were named beneficiaries to a joint-survivor life insurance policy. Perpetual- or continuing-care programs exist, offered by animal shelters and other animal facilities across the United States. This trend is gaining momentum.

PerPETual Care

Perpetual care programs evolved in response to the need for long-term care of pets who survive after the death of an owner. Pet Estates in Melrose, New York, offers a unique environment for orphaned pets. Estate pets socialize and play outside. Playtime includes swimming, boating, hiking, and many other outdoor or inside activities. Human senior citizens receive special invitations to pop in, since the facility believes visits provide good therapy to both pets and seniors.

The unusual facility sits above a pond, and provides a pet-safe environment with enclosed porches, living quarters, and play areas. Believe it or not, pet television and videos, music, and heated beds are standard amenities. Optional services include pet massage to relieve stress, muscle aches, and joint stiffness, and to aid circulation. Grooming is provided, and a veterinarian remains on-site at all times.

The College of Veterinary Medicine at the University of Minnesota also offers a PerPETual care program. Pet owners pay an enrollment fee and then make a minimum charitable bequest to the college. If the donor dies before his or her pet, the college finds a foster home and covers costs of medical care and food for the rest of the critter's life.

At the Stevenson Companion Animal Life Care Center run by Texas A&M University, orphaned pets have benefited from pet endowments for over a decade. Some owners make donations up front; others make bequests through a will or trust. Private facilities also provide such services.

PART FIVE
Grave Topics
at Tails End

The Natural History Museum in Los Angeles estimates that the inclusion of pets in human burials began between 14,000 and 9,000 years ago. One example of such archaeological evidence is a 12,000-year-old Natufian burial site (Israel) where a person was found buried with a puppy. But animals were not always buried with humans.

According to Salima Ikram, an Egyptologist with the Cairo Museum, animal mummification in Egypt reached its pinnacle of popularity during its 26th dynasty (664–525 B.C.E.). Initially, birds, monkeys, cats, dogs, gazelles, and other creatures were mummified and interred in the tombs of their owners. Later, many creatures were also entombed along the Nile within animal-specific burial grounds. Some even warranted their own tombs.

The sacred animal necropolis at Saqqara revealed the remains of nearly one million mummified creatures. Other sites at Abydos and Thebes also served as necropolises for a variety of creatures. At the time the baboon, ibis, cat, bull, and crocodile were considered sacred living avatars of Egyptian gods and so warranted placement in tombs or within underground cemeteries. These practices contrasted with companion animals whose final resting places consisted of coffins positioned adjacent to family plots.

Mummification continued until the spread of Christianity caused a decline in the ritual. God's creatures became persecuted as agents of evil and companions of witches. This maltreatment directly contrasted with centuries of affiliation and favor that existed in the pagan cults. Little tolerance existed for animal burials and pet bereavement ceremonies in the Christian era.

Interestingly enough, mummification and preservation practices are currently experiencing a resurgence in the United States. This coincides with a rise in other compassionate practices related to pet care, particularly those related to end-of-life care.

Critter Cremation

Jumbo, a celebrity elephant owned by P.T. Barnum, was mounted and displayed at Tufts University after his untimely death when a freight train collided with him. The stuffed behemoth became an unlikely mascot to Tufts' students until a fire destroyed his remains in the mid-1970s. Immediately after the blaze, some of his ashes were collected and placed within the confines of a peanut butter jar. Still housed there, they continue to serve as a good luck charm for Tufts athletic teams.

Jumbo's remains are a treasured memento of a majestic creature. Today, individual pet owners find the same solace in maintaining the cremains of departed companion animals. As society becomes increasingly mobile, and space progressively more limited, cremation becomes an attractive choice for many pet owners.

PET MEMORIAL

The sorrow of this physical loss weighs like an anchor, heavy on our hearts.

Our eyes flood with tears those times when we miss (pet's name) the most. Beyond our human experience, we know this pet now soars with the angels in realms we too shall one day roam.

We recognize the existence of deep, unconditional love and acceptance.

But even so, the physical passing of a being so dear to us is devastating; the soul and spirit that touched ours so deeply is sorely missed.

As we pray for understanding and healing, a message is revealed:

Each life has a profound impact on all others it touches.

As we move through the heartache, we move closer to embodying the peace that comes from knowing that his/her unique spark ignited the hearts of others and catalyzed changes beyond our wildest dreams.

As tears cleanse and heal our hearts and souls, they become symbolic drops of rain, gently falling and touching the ground where this pet sowed so many seeds.

The earth that seems so barren now will again sprout with new growth.

Those seedlings will mature and produce fruit of (pet's name)'s influence.

Its leaves will reflect light up to heaven, toward him/her.
We know (pet's name) will live forever in our hearts.
Each time the wind caresses and stirs the leaves, may
we think of him/her continuing in spirit, dancing
in that breeze that whispers to us all.

✦ ✦ ✦

BANGKOK CREMATION 🌿 In Bangkok, Thailand, a Buddhist temple in suburban Klongotey provides cremation services for pets. Pet owners bring deceased pets, and the temple provides flowers, incense, and candles. A cremation oven was specifically built for animals by order of the abbot. If desired, a monk prays in front of the chamber.

Crypt Comedy

With a twist of humor, Bert & Bud's Vintage Coffins says, "Don't be caught dead without one" (of their distinctive custom urns or coffins). The firm provides original works for the remains of deceased loved ones. In fact, when Mac, the beloved cat of Bud's wife passed on, Bud constructed a unique urn to hold the cremains.

The cat, rescued from the parking lot of a McDonald's® franchise, is memorialized in an urn sitting on top of two golden arches. The feline's favorite toy serves as the handle.

Custom-made caskets are available to anyone. Examples include a heart-shaped memorial and a festive urn fashioned for a beloved cat named for dancer Carmen Miranda (famous for her fruit-adorned headwear). This uniquely carved urn is painted in flashy colors and sits atop a pedestal of bananas!

PRAYER AFTER PET LOSS

(Pet's name) was a living blessing.

His/Her presence brought joy and light into our home,
to our friends, and to our family.

Although we are sad at the loss of his/her physical self,
the memories will live with us forever.

Those recollections will continue to bring smiles to our
faces, and warm our hearts.

(Pet's name), we thank God for bringing you into this
world and into our lives.

The joy and companionship of an animal is unparalleled,
and you have deeply touched us.

We will never forget you and pray that we see you again
in another place, another time.

Deadly Plots

A variety of tributes to departed pets exist around the globe. During the Chinese dynasties a dog cemetery was maintained in Peking, complete with tombstones constructed from marble, ivory, gold, and silver. Other established pet cemeteries existed in Paris, London, Edinburgh, Algiers, and St. Petersburg.

The evolution of pet cemeteries emerged from the love of pets, but also out of necessity. At one time, humans dwelling in densely populated areas threw deceased pets out with the trash, or the remains were placed in weighted sacks and dumped into a nearby river. Records indicate that when sanitation crews cleared it in 1899, the Seine River in Paris yielded the decaying remains of 3,000 deceased pets.

Opened in the summer of 1899, one of the first modern cemeteries was founded at Asnieres, near Paris, by lawyer George Harmios and journalist Marguerite Durand. The *"Société Française Anonyme du Cimetière Pour Chiens et Autre Animaux Domestiques"* (Nameless French Society for the Cemetery for Dogs and Other Pets) was later renamed *"Cimetière des Chiens d'Asnières"* (Dog Cemetery of Asnieres). Divided into three species-specific areas, the facility provided a mixed animal section with options for a mass grave or individual interment. This resting place for pets provides a peaceful garden setting and is the burial ground for celebrity dog actor Rin-Tin-Tin.

PET BEREAVEMENT PRAYER

Today we gather in sorrow over the loss of (pet's name).
Beyond this realm is spirit, and we affirm that life
  is eternal.

Before birth and after death is another existence.
Let us remember this and so be reassured.
Our love for (pet's name) is eternal, unceasing.
Our physical separation is painful, temporary.
Comfort us, bestow peace and healing.
And let us celebrate this beloved creature's memory.

✦ ✦ ✦

American Plotters

One late night in 1898, Mrs. Chevalier of Columbus, Ohio, secretly entered a human cemetery to conduct a burial service for her little dog. Other desperate pet owners followed suit, burying pets in family plots. Urban life and intense bonds with animals created a demand for a new service, pet cemeteries.

The first animal cemeteries in western society began appearing in the late nineteenth century. The Hartsdale Pet Cemetery in New York is the oldest operating cemetery in America. Established in 1896 by Dr. Samuel Johnson, a prominent Manhattan veterinarian, the grounds are manicured, and artistically crafted gravestones mark many graves. Hartsdale contains an area for communal burial known as the Peaceable Kingdom. The facility also conducts an annual memorial service for veteran war dogs.

Burial traditions at this facility also range from simple to elaborate. The Walsh Mausoleum is a granite structure weighing more than 50 tons; not far away is a life-size stone doghouse marking the grave of Buster, a dog who died in 1942.

Burial traditions of pets depend on the ethnic and religious affinity of owners. Many copy funeral traditions of humans. Obituaries appear in daily newspapers for humans, but pet obituaries and condolences usually find their way into special publications for pets, on virtual memorial sites, or in other creative venues.

Last rites for pets can be as formal as any for humans. In the Victorian era, deceased critters were photographed in the same manner as deceased children. Many pet owners kept lockets containing fur and other keepsakes in memory of those dearly departed. Today's memorials return to similar practices.

Pet Eulogy Service

Select meaningful music and form a circle around the burial ground or area the ashes will be scattered. Conduct this service at sunset to represent passing on or at sunrise to symbolize new beginnings.

*We respectfully call in the Great Spirit. Essences of
the earth and sky, we ask you to receive our beloved
(pet's name).
May his/her remains contribute to the circle of life.
Enfold us in compassion.
Bond us during this difficult time.
Reveal the lessons needed to assist our understanding.
Shift our perspective over this loss.*

All join hands. The officiant directs those gathered to breathe meditatively.

*Life begins with a deep breath and ends with an exhale.
Breathe now and inhale love and light.
Allow fond memories of this departed love one to fill any
aching or empty space.
Breathe out and release sorrow and grief.
In your mind's eye witness the light of this bright spirit
moving into another realm without pain, without
reservation.*

Light a candle or acknowledge the sun or moon through gesture or movement.

> *Let go and send blessings to (pet's name).*
> *When the sun sets, the moon rises and the reflective*
>   *glow continues.*
> *So will it be with this being who added luster to this*
>   *world and who will continue to light our lives through*
>   *fond contemplation.*
> *As the sun rises, let us remember that after each ending*
>   *is a new beginning.*
> *Memories of this being will illuminate the darkness.*
> *Allow (pet's name)'s soft afterglow to engulf us.*
> *May we find peace.*

Cast flower petals or place flowers on gravesite.

> *Through each season there is transition and so it is in life.*
> *Life begins with a seed, grows and blossoms, withers, dies,*
>   *and cycles again.*
> *Feel free to share a story or memory of (pet's name).*
> *When finished, cast your flower in memory of the beauty*
>   *in life and how it continues.*

Sprinkle water or symbolically incorporate water in the ceremony.

> *These tears drop to the earth cleansing our pain, releasing*
> *our sorrow, just as the rain douses the earth, quenches*
> *the terrain, travels on a journey to the sea, and evaporates.*
> *This passage reminds us again of the circle of life, ever*
> *changing, ever present.*
> *Let us be cleansed and allow (pet's name) to transition*
> *to other realms, in another form.*

Scatter earth or ashes.

> *Over time, the rocks, trees, plants, and animals transition,*
> *absorbed by the earth.*
> *Dust blows over the desert, mud moves mountainsides,*
> *and sand travels great distances to other shores.*
> *As we scatter this earth/these ashes we acknowledge that*
> *we shall again feel our feet on solid ground and*
> *remember that (pet's name) has embarked on a new*
> *journey to other destinations.*
> *May his/her travels be sanctified.*
> *Keep us centered in faith and grounded as we travel*
> *through life from this time forward.*

Fishy Funeral

Flushing fish is passé. For those with long-living water companions, creative ideas literally spark unique ceremonials. When beloved goldfish Geisha passed on, family members wanted to honor her in a light fashion.

So, they shaped a seaworthy craft out of balsa wood decorated with flowers and a black sail. Geisha's body was wrapped in tissue and place upon the vessel. Finally, the family gathered on the shore of the community lake, shared fond memories about the bold beauty, and ignited the ferry. As they pushed it away from shore, wishes for a happy journey filled the air.

This family believes that the symbolic farewell ceremony transformed the loss process for their children, who did not suffer nightmares or other emotional outbursts afterward. The experiences gleaned by witnessing a voyage into new realms yielded memories that honored the passing of a living creature and granted permission to grieve the loss. These expressions nurtured and enhanced healing.

FISH PRAYER

Ashes to ashes,
Dust to dust,
May this critter go where dead fish must.
And even though this loss is to our dismay,
We know we shall see him/her again some day.

Tails of Devotion

Pet memorials can be as unique as a family desires to make them. Work together to establish something to help process grief and to memorialize the animal in a distinctive and personal manner.

Collage

It's quite easy to create collages. Copy favorite photos and create a scrapbook of memories or a unique wall display to honor the life of the pet and all the great things he or she added to life. Don't limit the collection to just pictures or drawings. Include pet tags, baby teeth, favorite remnants of toys, and other unique additions.

Photo Memorial

Commemorate a beloved pet with a photographic memorial and decorate the matting around it. Place favorite snapshots so they surround the urn. Consider scattering cremains in the animal's favorite spot. Take care to allow the ashes to remain in the home until every family member is ready to release them.

Scrapbook

Scrapbooking is a favorite pastime for many families. It's best to begin constructing a pet book early in the pet's life so the scrapbook includes a multitude of mementos and follows the animal's entire lifespan. Working on such a project after the death of a companion animal helps survivors of loss process grief. It can be especially beneficial and healing for children. Ask youngsters to draw pictures, write poems, or share memories, and encourage them to express their feelings of loss.

Flower Petals

Ritual celebrations help many people acknowledge and deal with the loss so they can let go. Dry flowers from a memorial service for display or make them into a potpourri mix. Annual memorial celebrations help some people. Flower petals may be scattered symbolically in representation of emotional release.

Share Joyful Memories

Although the loss of a pet is incredibly painful, it helps to share happy memories. As friends and family share stories, record them into an audio file. Photographs and videos of the pet during favorite outings and activities can turn into a short composite tribute to his or her life. Hire a professional to edit clips into an attractive musical and visual memorial.

Candle

Keep a candle lit in honor of the pet and let its brilliance symbolize the joy and light the animal added to life. The illuminating glow the flame casts represents the ethereal light of the pet's existence beyond this realm.

Memorial Tree

Many people sow living plants or trees in honor of animals. The seed sprouting into new life is a reminder that life continues through transitions. For those without a yard or window garden, it is possible to create a memorial using silk flowers and plants.

GUARDIAN PET PRAYER
by the Anglican Society for the Welfare of Animals
O Lord, give us humility to thank You for the creation
of animals, who can show affection which sometimes
puts us to shame.

Enlarge our respect for these your creatures, of whom
we are the guardian.

And give us a sense of responsibility toward all your
creation, for Jesus Christ's sake.

Amen.

Creature Comforts

Most people do not know how to assist their friends during a time of grief. Pet bereavement remains a tough process for animal lovers. Although some obtain another animal quickly, many will not.

When Beverly put down her beloved dog, friends showed up for the euthanasia, which the veterinarian conducted at Beverly's home. Under the pines, Bev held the head of her cherished canine as he took his last breath. Afterward, Beverly couldn't walk. Hands supported and guided her inside. The dog's empty shell remained outside; overcome with grief, Bev couldn't function or deal with the loss.

Doug, a neighbor, graciously delivered the canine's body to the crematorium and handled all arrangements. In fact, he later journeyed several hours to pick up the cremains. This charitable act embossed a lasting memory of kindness on her heart. Nothing made Bev's process easier or lessened her pain. Even so, the memory endures of incredible kindness and the compassionate people who made themselves available to her during that dire time in her life.

Unfortunately, most people have no idea what actions to take to help someone survive the crisis of loss. Believe it or not, the simplest of acts often mean the most. Offering condolences and assistance is a great way to start.

Some people appreciate receiving home-cooked meals, while others just need a hand to hold, or a kind, listening ear. Deep loss requires compassion, not much else, so always ask what people need. They may share or they may not, but caring efforts always help.

In some cases, a movie or book on tape may be able to provide a good distraction. Quiet company is also often appreciated. Invitations for activities or outings might not be accepted but usually are valued, so don't hesitate to offer.

TIMELESS TRADITIONS ❧ Richard Chalfen, of Temple University in Pennsylvania, found the Japanese keep grave pictures called *"doubutsu no haka no shashin"* in the *"butsudan"* (household altar). Dedicated to recently deceased family members, these pictures also include animals. Different practices exist. Some Buddhist sects believe animals are reincarnations of their great ancestors. Chalfen said, "For this reason, owners of the pet cannot let others take care of their pet after it dies. They think that an evil spell will be cast upon the family if they don't bury animals properly."

When he visited a pet cemetery section of Jindaiji (a temple built in 733 C.E.), Chalfen saw blessing requests for animals, lanterns decorated with astrological signs, pleas to the goddess of mercy, and commemoration sticks called *tooma* inscribed with pet names. The *tooma* signal visits of pet masters to particular gravesites. Photos of deceased pets are secured to them by visiting pet owners.

PRAYER FOR COMFORT

Shower us with compassion.

Envelop us in the warmth of healing energy.

Today we entreat you to welcome (pet's name) into
    your arms.

Although we miss his/her joyful presence, warm breath,
    and physical touch, we know that (pet's name) now
    joins your choir of creatures.

As his/her voice joins the symphony in heaven, we ask
    to hear the resounding joy, to feel the blissful vibration,
    and so take comfort in knowing that all is well.

✦ ✦ ✦

Dead Pets Society

In the United Kingdom, the *Independent* reported an increase in pet burials, with an estimated 140,000 pet funerals held in the area every year. Indicators of this increasing trend include specialty services and products specifically for pet burials such as biodegradable coffins, a funeral ceremony book, and unique pet grave markers on which it is possible to etch a pet's name.

American entrepreneurs, who lead the pet funerary trend, now provide not only unique products and services for such loss, but also personalized support services on request. Pet Memories, a pet burial and cremation service in Iowa, searched for a groomer in response to a client's request for one last pet makeover before the animal's burial.

PRAYER AT THE LOSS
OF A BELOVED PET

Dear Heavenly Host,

We come to you today with heavy hearts.

Immerse us in your light and love.

*Assist us in healing from the loss of our beloved
    (pet's name).*

*We give thanks for the many blessings this animal
    has bestowed upon our family.*

*Please welcome our pet into your arms and watch
    after him/her until we meet again.*

*Lift our spirits and replace our sorrow with joyful
    memories of our lives together.*

We know that as we ask, we shall receive.

Amen.

Funerary Gems

At the moment, Chicago, Illinois, offers the most avant-garde options for addressing pet loss. LifeGem,® a company established in 2001, turns cremated remains of a loved one into a gemstone. The premise is simple; every living creature is a carbon-based life form, so why not turn it into a memorable, individualized, and beautiful keepsake? So for several thousand dollars LifeGem® "turns a man's best friend into a girl's best friend."

Want to plot an afterlife together with a pet? Another Chicago business offers a way for pets and owners to spend eternity with each other. To get around the long-standing cemetery bylaws restricting burial practices to humans only, Memorial Traditions offers distinct pet-owner cemeteries within two existing graveyards, Eden Park and Schiller Park.

In the past, human cemeteries and pet graveyards existed separately. To keep traditionalists happy, the firm established specific areas within the larger site to accommodate pets and owners. For an additional fee, family plots house both humans and furry, feathered, finned, or scaly companions. Pets usually pass away first, so they are placed deep within the gravesite. When the owner dies, he or she is buried a few feet above.

Oreo, a beloved family guinea pig, was buried in Eden Park. The moving burial service proved significant to family members, especially for the adolescent child who tossed the first handful of dirt onto the grave. Some family friends shake their heads in disbelief over such efforts, while others support their choice and ponder the idea themselves.

PRAYER FOR FLORA AND FAUNA

We pray for the flora and fauna of this world.
May all thrive and flourish.
Remind us to care for all living things.
Increase our bonds with the beasts, wild and tame.
Impart tenderness in the hearts of humans toward all
*   our animal relations.*
May we evolve into the stewards they need.
Allow us to become astute students to their teachings
*   and examples.*
Let us become one with all creation and rejoice in that
*   connection.*

PART SIX

Pet-Pourri

The Ten Commandments of Successful Animal Ceremonies
Can planners create a ceremony that presents a peaceable kingdom?
Can they avoid critter chaos at pet events? The answer is yes! Amazingly, animal blessings rarely encounter problems. But to avoid a real
zoo, abide by the Ten Commandments.

CREATURE CEREMONY COMMANDMENTS

Thou shall provide shade.

*Thou shall provide safe transport and use proper
restraining devices while attending an event.*

Thou shall provide water and receptacles for drinking.

*Thou shall provide (and guide pets to use) pet toileting
areas and clean-up equipment.*

*Thou shall be a responsible pet handler and not allow
altercations between animals.*

Thou shall mind thy owner.

Thou shall not nip, claw, or kick.

Thou shall not urinate except in designated areas.
Thou shall not run amuck.
Thou shall behave and get along with others.

✦ ✦ ✦

These Ten Commandments of Animal Ceremonies start the adventure. Make each event as distinctive as the organization or individual holding the gala. Many facilities hold pet blessings, bark mitzvahs, and other festivities as fund-raisers; gatherings can be great social occasions and meaningful ongoing celebrations.

Animals remain an extension of the family, and blessings begin by giving thanks to them for their many contributions. Animals labor for humans, provide food, and offer companionship. In the past, blessings were often for the fertility and continued health of the animals. Pet blessings now resemble ceremonies to bless children.

Usually pets receive a blessing from a spiritual leader. In some cases, this section of the ceremony includes a sprinkling of holy water. In others, actions include only a simple pat on the head, a hand suspended above the pet, or a hand casually placed on the animal while a blessing is recited.

At non-religious events, instead of prayers, a reading from favorite animal passages, collection of poetry, or speech is appropriate. The point is to celebrate the human-animal bond and animal contributions.

Successful affairs require planning. The choice to hold one indoors or outside remains a matter of preference or weather conditions. Larger events tend to take place outdoors, where people gather in waiting areas or amble in the surroundings. Some festivities include vendors or entertainment.

Smaller gatherings don't require as much energy, but planning is essential so the celebration is fun and safe. Most people convince friends or neighbors to help with smaller occasions, but for larger endeavors, seek out pooch planners, pet-friendly ministers or other animal-loving spiritual leaders, and dedicated volunteers.

Plan ahead, so little overlooked areas reveal themselves. Ponder whether to advertise or send invitations. Invitations can be purchased or handmade. Local media outlets, receptive to press releases, often turn up to cover events. However, attract more people by advertising through local outlets and via flyers or banners.

Most religious centers and municipal agencies already provide insurance for assemblies, but check to see. Other locations may require additional coverage. Verify that policies cover pet-related challenges.

Each animal can react differently but most clergy report that animals settle down for blessings, although a few get a bit feisty or vocal when they receive a splatter of holy water. My personal observations verify that animals quiet down and behave courteously. Out of hundreds or thousands of animals attending events, only an occasional delinquent dog or felonious feline acts up, and only occasionally will a bird fly the coop.

Twenty Tips for Successful Pet Blessings

1. Decide whether an indoor or outdoor location is best for the event.

Avoid inclement weather and provide services for a small gathering using indoor locations. The benefits include little worry about climate and optimal privacy.

Larger gatherings are best held in outdoor settings. The most popular locations include yards or grounds of the facility. Outdoor locations allow flexibility for staging and set-up; they accommodate vendors and house entertainers, and allow greater numbers of supporters and spectators to attend. When setting up the location, provide shaded areas for waiting, and rope off toileting areas for pets. Don't forget to include clean-up aids.

UNIQUE TWISTS 🌿 In Santa Ana, California, St. Anne's School decided drive-thru divinity provided a better, safer way to deal with pets and owners. To do something similar requires a good-size parking lot, temperate weather, and a system for directing traffic. Be innovative!

---

2. Set arrival times, event phases, and an end time.

It is essential to schedule set-up times and volunteer arrival periods. Participants often arrive very early, so provide gathering areas. Schedule an end time along with the beginning. This is critical for contributing vendors and other organizations. Once established, stick to the original schedule. Most services last 30–40 minutes, followed immediately by individual blessings and other activities. Festivities can continue all day.

3. Include entertainment or activities.

Many people enjoy spending the day with pets and look forward to reasons to stay on-site. Provide booth spaces for animal groups, clubs, and unique vendors that can enhance the visitors' experience.

Musicians are always a plus, but keep it to quieter types such as acoustical guitarists, flutists, and more harmonious melodies. It is true that music soothes the savage beast but strive to supply a relaxing atmosphere for people, too.

Most coordinators suggest keeping blessing ceremonies non-commercial by inviting educational groups. Other than food vendors, larger gatherings concentrate on creating goodwill and leave the fund-raising to different activities. Provide a donation box for those who want to contribute. A guest book helps reconnect with participants at a later date. Don't forget to use this tool to invite them to another animal blessing.

4. Invite friends or support services and businesses to attend.

Successful blessing events include neighborhood residents and friends. Invite such participants as the mounted police, rescue dogs, therapy animals, trick riders, and animal control personnel.

In addition, local pet stores, pet product manufacturers, animal shelters, rescue agencies, and breed clubs often make enthusiastic participants. Many of those agencies encourage their supporters and members to attend, since it gives them an opportunity to showcase their products and services.

5. Designate special areas for waiting, toileting, or social activities.
Pet staging area essentials include shade and seating for attendees. Ideal toileting area locations include easy access from adjacent waiting areas and center of activities. Make staging viewable from any location. Position vendors around the perimeter so they don't block views. This also prevents traffic flow from clogging the main location.

6. Provide tools to assist visitors.
Popular necessities include water bowls and the means and volunteers to fill them. Other requirements consist of pooper scoops, gloves, poop bags, and special waste dumpsters. A disinfectant bucket for scoopers is optional. If desired, place it adjacent to waste receptacles but make sure it is high enough to prevent pets from drinking out of it.

Place pet poop scoop bag dispensers in strategic places as a visual reminder. Since municipal districts furnish public dispensers for pet owners, contact them for supplier information. Shovels and lime may be necessary for large animal waste. Remember, toileting regions function best when located on perimeter areas.

7. Set parameters and rules in advance.
Managing large groupings of animals is a combination of luck and planning. Safety guidelines are part of this effort. Stage hooved or livestock animals away from dogs and cats. House birds and small

mammals in cages or containers to prevent escape and offer protection. Carriers and leashes or harnesses should be required for all animals. Dictate that unusual critters, such as pigs or exotic animals, be housed in appropriate caging, wagons, or in carriages.

Problems arise, so remember to get creative. Monsignor Paul Martin has blessed his share of animals over the past thirteen years. The St. Anne's chaplain officiated over events originally held on a field nearby; disobedient dogs catalyzed a change to drive-thru blessings. The decision was made for safety and convenience, and to avoid the "dog park gone wild" challenges previously encountered.

People with unruly pets or sick companion animals can participate in animal blessing by bringing pictures of their critters. Many bring stuffed animals or similar representatives for pets. When promoting the blessing, highlight these options so everyone feels comfortable attending, even if pets cannot.

Finally, review any liability insurance. Many churches and business policies include special coverage, but make sure. Call local insurance agency representatives with questions about coverage well in advance.

8. Choose between a processional or individual visitations.

Although many clergy meander through crowds, the preferred method of animal blessing is first to recite a group blessing, followed by a procession past clergy for individual blessings. An elevated stage or platform provides additional safety and ease of access. Some choose to have animals remain in place while clergy navigate to them or station clergy at specific locations and allow animals to parade past.

9. Provide some sort of blessing memento.

Special touches include certificates or participant ribbons, party favors, and even recipes. Many gift these items to participants. Sell small St. Francis medallions for pet collars or special bandanas to raise funds.

10. Request animal service officers attend.

Invite local animal services personnel to participate. Animal control officers and mounted police assist with public education and safety. Additionally, these professionals help monitor the area, prevent incidents, and assist in emergencies.

11. Visit other locations to glean tips and get a feel for what to expect.

Attend animal blessings and similar functions to view management and structure. Visiting actual events provides a real sense of what is appealing and what challenges to anticipate, and reveals additional ideas.

12. Provide parking passes for vendors and assistants.

Depending on the facility, plan to apportion specific parking for vendors and assistants. Easy loading and unloading of booths or supplies is critical and is essential for traffic regulation and flow. Keep specific areas open for emergency access.

13. Provide an information center for vendors and visitors.

Set up a specific location for check-in. Include a map, and post the schedule in an information booth. Ease of access allows vendors and visitors to glean vital information and cuts down on personnel needs. The site is also ideal for dispensing certificates and other goodies.

Information boards and volunteers at strategic locations make it easier to monitor activities and provide direction. Gather names and addresses for drawings to build a mailing list, or give out special ribbons so an estimate of attendance is available.

14. Communications

Designate a clear channel of communication using cell phones or hand-held radio communication devices. Develop protocols for crisis situations, and identify volunteers with bandanas or unique identifying clothing and badges.

15. Offer Activities

For long events, provide activities for kids such as mask-making. Ask local community theater groups to dress up and provide "animal antics" to entertain the crowd. Use imagination!

16. Provide security and off-limit areas for dignitaries and celebrities.

Designate a specific place where attending dignitaries or celebrities can escape the public. Assign an escort to assist notables to and from the festivities. Some dignitaries arrive with private security personnel. Arrange for the event coordinator to interface with them to synchronize efforts.

17. Dictate costumes be left at home.

To avoid friction at religious-oriented ceremonies or sacred events, instruct attendees to refrain from dressing up in costume or inappropriate attire. Exceptions to the rule are groomed animals, pets dressed up for the occasion, and hired performers. Suggest guidelines to the audience beforehand.

18. After clean-up, celebrate with catered food or a potluck for volunteers and vendors.

Hardworking volunteers and vendors enjoy rewards for all their hard work and diligence. Feeding the work force goes over big. Don't forget to invite participant families. If you're throwing a potluck, ask those not working during the festivities to contribute, but allow those who did toil to attend without bringing a dish.

19. Take photos.

Encourage shutterbugs to take photos to start an archive. Photographs help during future promotions. Sell duplicate photos as an additional fund-raiser after the occasion.

20. Enjoy!

Finally, take a few moments to enjoy the blessing. Schedule breaks in the day to bask in the delightful festivities.

BLESS THE BEASTS

We send thanks to our companion animals, domestic livestock, and pets.

Spirit, teach us to have compassion, give us kind words, enable us to gently handle these beloved beasts.

We give thanks for the insects that ride on the currents of air, creep and crawl above and below the soil, and that buzz in the shadows of the majestic trees and provide so many services to all. Grand are the insect and arachnid cleanup crews who remove the lifeless debris and assist in the recycling process.

We appreciate the beauty of the butterfly and the song of the crickets and ask for blessing for all the bugs and worms for their vital roles in this web of life. Help all see their uniqueness and escalate human appreciation for them.

We give thanks for the winged wonders of the sky, avian clans of the water, and the fowl of the earth. Their beauty, songs, and grace fill our lives and help our spirits soar. May our hearts flutter in joy with the beat of their wings. Keep our birdie brethren in insects and seeds. May their nestlings be healthy and fit and may they all enjoy full lives.

We send blessings to our reptilian relatives and ask that understanding and appreciation replace fear and mistrust. May we recognize and be grateful for the

diverse roles these scaled associates play. May we
see the unique splendor of those who crawl, slither,
and scamper.

We thank those of the forest, field, meadows, and desert
for gracing our lives. Their wildness calls out to us
and lures us to venture into new terrain.

We send thanks also to the creatures of the sea and
water. They inspire us to embark deep into uncharted
territory and challenge us to expand our senses.

May we continue to cherish the large and the small, the
predator and prey, and may blessings fill the lives of
all beasts.

✦ ✦ ✦

To obtain additional tips and hints and to receive a special bonus
for *Blessing of the Animals* readers, please visit www.blessingofthe
animals.com and enter promotional code 06DGBA0411.

ACKNOWLEDGMENTS

Book birthing relies on a multitude of talented people. The extensive process begins with an idea. As it gestates, slowly developing into a unique personality, the physical attributes change until it eventually takes final form, at last arriving for all to see. During the long, arduous process, many interviews, submissions, and discussions occur.

Not everyone or everything makes it into the final product. This list of acknowledgments mentions only the names of those contributors and unfaltering supporters who were with me at the end of the process. To all those not listed and to any who might be omitted unintentionally, I extend my profound gratitude for your time, talents, passion, and humor.

To my agent, Sheree Bykofsky and the staff at Bykofsky & Associates, *merci beaucoup* for your advocacy, support, insight, and savvy. You remain an awesome blessing to me.

To Hannah Reich, Leigh Ann Ambrosi, and the capable team at Sterling Publishing, thank you for partnering with me on this beautiful venture. For visionary alignment on the project, and for compassionate support when the darkness of inconceivable loss surrounded me, Jo Fagan, words cannot express my thanks.

For awesome guidance, instruction, and tools, my heartfelt appreciation goes to Annie Jennings and Tony Trupiano; your innovative generosity over the years remains unparalleled.

Foundational friendships supported this project from inception, and I cannot imagine life without their affection, generosity, humor, and support. So I am grateful to Rev. Elivia Melodey, Lee Födi, Rita S. Robinson-Campbell, Paula Porter, Stephanie Jefferson, Tom Averill, and Raymond Martin. To book maven and buddy, Lindsay Johnson, thanks for your wit, wisdom, and laughter.

An honorable mention goes to those cheerleaders who incessantly asked about this project and who make me feel truly loved. The squad includes Moose Lodge 2085, the townsfolk of Fawnskin, numerous residents of the Big Bear Valley, and my loyal electronic newsletter subscribers from around the world.

To friends and editors Susan Chan, Nancy Lucas, and Don Plemmons, bless you for understanding my hiatus prior to book deadline.

Last, but not least, enormous gratitude to those who willingly shared their time, stories, and resources to make this book a unique and joyful process. Individuals and institutions include:

Anglican Society for the Welfare of Animals: Samantha Chandler, Linda J. Bodicoat, and staff.

Author and friend Robena Grant.

Cathedral of Saint John the Divine: Reverend Storm Swain and Harold Katz.

Chosencouture.com: Sara Schwimmer.

Duke Chapel: DeRonda Elliott, Robin Argus, Craig Kocher.

Grace Episcopal Church: Reverend Julie Norton and Cynthia Arnold.

Hartsdale Pet Cemetery: Edward Martin III.

Hendrix College: Jay McDaniel.

Holy Spirit Catholic Church: Monsignor Allen Roy.

Hymns & Hounds: Reverend Dee Renda.

Mt. Pleasant Animal Shelter: Nicole Drummond and
Rachel Rothrock.

Nikki Hospice for Pets: Kathryn Marocchino.

Olvera Street: Emily Martinez, Connie Ramirez, Diana Robertson,
Zorthian Family, the merchants, personnel, and volunteers at
El Pueblo's Blessing of the Animals.

Our Lady Queen of Angels Church: Father Steve Niskanen, CMF.

Photographer and animal enthusiast Kilbee Brittain.

Rancher and cowgirl poet Yvonne Hollenbeck.

Saint Bartholomew Catholic Church: Monsignor Sean B. Flanagan.

Saint Boniface Church & St. Anthony Foundation:
Fr. Floyd A. Lotito, OFM.

Saint Francis Episcopal Church: Reverend Mark Lingle.

Southwestern University: Dr Laura Hobgood-Oster.

Stephen Huneck Gallery & Dog Chapel: Stephen & Gwen Huneck.

Tuft's University and Harvard University: Paul Waldau.

Weddings Performed: Minister Lynn Turner.

All prayers and ceremonies are by Diana L. Guerrero unless noted otherwise.

Page 13: *Animal Awareness Blessing* used by kind permission of the Anglican Society for the Welfare of Animals

Page 13: *Sermon to the Birds* by Saint Francis of Assisi

Page 18: *Blessing for the Animals* as recited by Cardinal Roger Michael Mahony, from the 76th anniversary of Olvera Street's blessing of the animals

Page 21: *Prayer of St. Francis*

Page 23: *Prayer for Blessing of the Animals* by Monsignor Sean Flanagan

Page 25: *Duke Chapel Blessing* © Duke University Chapel

Page 26: *Creature Blessing* as recited by Father Floyd A. Lotito

Page 29: *Nature's Church* © Yvonne Hollenbeck

Page 34: *Thanksgiving Blessing* by the Reverend Julie Norton

Pages 36–37: *Prayer for Animal Welfare Sunday* used by kind permission of The Anglican Society for the Welfare of Animals and by kind permission of Ms. Linda J Bodicoat

Page 75: *Candlemas Day*

Page 103: *Guardian Pet Prayer* used by kind permission of the Anglican Society for the Welfare of Animals

ABOUT THE AUTHOR

Diana L. Guerrero's first word was "fish," which proved prophetic of her future life and occupation with animals. Pet owners, zoos, and other domestic and exotic animal facilities call upon this author, professional speaker, and animal coach for her expertise and knowledge.

Guerrero's diverse career spans over thirty years. She has been affiliated with the San Diego Wild Animal Park, the Los Angeles Zoo, the Cabrillo Marine Aquarium, Marineland, the Humboldt Wildlife Rehabilitation Center, and many private collections, humane agencies, shelters, community dog-training programs, private pet owners, grooming salons, and other agencies. An innovative leader, she has also conducted classes for many institutions, including the largest adult education program provider in the United States, the Learning Annex.

In addition to her practical experience and natural aptitude with animals, Guerrero has attended and completed courses in both animal management and training in the United States and Europe. She is an alumna of the Moorpark College Exotic Animal Training & Management Program, Ralph Helfer's Gentle Jungle Affection Training School, the International Training Centre at the Durrell Wildlife Conservation Trust, and special program extensions with Marwell Zoological Park and Kent University in England. She also has numerous certifications in non-traditional fields, such as animal disaster preparedness and Reiki.

This gifted trainer's vast experience also includes a long list of media appearances, including the *Today Show*, National Public Radio, Animal Planet®, the *Wall Street Journal*, the *Washington Post*, PBS's *Nature*, *Good Morning America*, *ABC News*, *NBC News*, and many more.

In addition to her columns and books, Guerrero publishes *Ark Animals*, an Internet magazine on animal behavior, pet training, unusual animal careers, and other topics.

Guerrero's unique adventures with animals of all types give her unparalleled experiences and insight, and her travels contribute to her knowledge about the many aspects and requirements of the animal field.

The "auntie" to a multitude of wild and domestic critters, Guerrero consults and trains animals in the spring and summer. In the fall and winter her favorite activities involve writing and adventuring in the snow-covered mountains where she lives. Her home attracts the creatures she so loves; raccoons frolic on her deck, squirrels scamper, coyotes trot down her stairs, and bird dramas are ever-occurring in the treetops around her. One Steller's jay seems to have a crush on Diana; if he can't see her, he hops around until he can locate her, or even pecks on the window to get her attention.

Visit www.arkanimals.com or www.dianalguerrero.com to contact the author and learn more.

INDEX